My Problems, God's Solutions

Property of Fred Tellerday
5816 Prunian Avenue
Lisle, Il 60532
630 - 964 - 0883

My Problems,
God's Solutions

George W. Fellendorf

Pleasant Word
A Division of WINEPRESS PUBLISHING

Pleasant Word (a division of WinePress Publishing, PO Box 428, Enumclaw, Washington 98022) functions only as book publisher. As such, the ultimate design, content, editorial accuracy, and views expressed or implied in this work are those of the author.

Unless otherwise noted, all Scriptures are taken from the Holy Bible, New International Version, Copyright © 1973, 1978, 1984 by the International Bible Society. Used by permission of Zondervan Publishing House. The "NIV" and "New International Version" trademarks are registered in the United States Patent and Trademark Office by International Bible Society.

ISBN 13: 978-1-4141-0913-8
ISBN 10: 1-4141-0913-X
Library of Congress Catalog Card Number: 2006910616

A summary of one man's experiences
in seeking and finding God's help
in meeting the needs of the day

Table of Contents

Foreword

Someone has said that life is a steady progression of steps toward death, beginning at conception and ending when the brain, lungs, and heart cease to function. Thus, death is the ultimate and inevitable solution to all of life's problems. The real question is what happens to us between conception and death and how do we handle it?

To the Christian, death is not the end but the beginning of a new life in the presence of God Himself. While progressing through our life on earth toward our ultimate transition to our heavenly home, however, we all must face physical, emotional, and spiritual problems. In the words of Oswald Chambers (*My Utmost for His Highest* [July 28]), "What we see as only the process in reaching a particular goal, God sees as the goal itself."

This little book is a review of one man's experiences over a lifetime of problems and solutions to problems as revealed by an almighty and loving Father.

Introduction

So I say to you: ask and it will be given to you; seek and you will find; knock and the door will be opened to you. For everyone who asks receives; he who seeks finds; and to him who knocks, the door will be opened. (Luke 11:9–10)

For I am convinced that neither death nor life, neither angels nor demons, neither the present or the future, nor any powers, neither height nor depth, nor anything else in all creation, will be able to separate us from the love of God that is in Christ Jesus our Lord. (Romans 8:38–39)

Have you ever tried to imagine what it would be like to have a loving, all-knowing, and ever-present father with whom you could discuss every issue that was important to you? And after listening patiently each time, he would reach out, take your hands into his, and say, "Now, let me give you exactly the right solution to whatever is of concern to you today"?

This book is about someone who has had access to such a father, twenty-four hours a day, seven days a week, for the last fifty years of his adult life. I know He was there for all of the other thirty years of my life too, but I cannot remember such an intimate relationship then as I will be describing in this book.

Too often we tend to turn to prayer only when we are facing a big problem and we don't know where else to turn for answers. Little problems seem to resolve themselves. The bigger problems often require more than we are offered by the usual sources, such as parents and friends.

Should prayer be the first or the last place to seek help? I would suggest from my experience that prayer should come at the very top of the list of sources of help for both large and small problems.

Of course, if things turn out the way we had hoped, we say, "Wasn't I lucky?" or "I really solved that problem, didn't I?" Frequently the word "coincidence" pops up, and the solution to a problem is credited to chance rather than the intervention of an almighty, loving God.

Oswald Chambers, in his book, *My Utmost for His Highest,* has said in his daily devotion for August 28: "You must give Jesus the opportunity and the room to work." The problem is that we will not do this until we are at our wits' end. As long as you think you are self-sufficient, you do not need to ask God for anything.

I write down my problems, large or small, on a small "My Problem Card" at the moment they arise. I have tried to make this the first step, not the last, in seeking help. I refer to these cards during my daily devotions when I am studying God's Word and praying for guidance.

I have found that daily Bible study, followed by prayer for understanding and guidance from the Holy Spirit, helps prepare me to first recognize, and then accept God's answers as they are revealed by the circumstances in my life. I cannot recommend too highly the practice of writing down your problems as they occur and then committing them to the Lord by physically placing a card in your personal Bible and asking for God's solution in prayer every day.

This is not an original idea. I first discovered My Problem Cards during a weekend visit to New York City in 1956, where Hazel and I went to celebrate our tenth wedding anniversary. We attended Sunday services at the Marble Collegiate Church where Norman Vincent Peale was pastor. My Problem Cards were in the pew racks at this historic old church (Figure 1).

I have found that God has responded to my requests for help with three basic types of answers: "Yes," "No," and "Not yet." In the pages that follow, I describe only a small sample of the hundreds of My Problem Cards that I have written over these years.

I must admit that I still have a few cards that have been answered "Not yet." Nonetheless, I continue to bring them to God's attention and look forward expectantly to the day when "Not yet" changes to "Yes" or "No." For some, I may have to wait until I am sitting at His feet to get the solutions.

Looking back on my My Problem Cards written over a period of fifty years, I have found it both helpful and inspiring to ask myself the following questions about each recorded situation. I would encourage readers to refer to these questions as they review my experience. Then, if you decide to begin using My Problem Cards yourself, ask these questions about your own experience with My Problem Cards in the future:

1. Were my prayers answered in exactly the way I expected? If not, do I now understand why God's way was better than my way?
2. Was the kingdom of God glorified and advanced by the way God answered my prayer?
3. Were my family and friends enlightened and strengthened by God's solution to my problem?
4. Looking back, did God know what He was doing; and, in His own time and in His own way, did He provide just the right solution to my problem?

Will you join me in this adventure in faith and trust?

A NOTE ON THE TEXT

In the following pages, the actual text as handwritten on the My Problem Cards is shown with the date it was written. The text in between describes the events, thoughts, and circumstances of my life before and after the cards were written.

MY PROBLEM

In getting an answer to a problem, it helps to write it down. This makes it specific, and you are better able to think it through and pray about it.

Write your problem on this card and date it. Place it in your personal Bible. Pray about it daily. Be ready and willing to accept God's answer.

Finally, note the day the answer is revealed and write it down on the other side of the card. Then file the card with praise and thanksgiving.

Date:

Figure 1

Chapter 1

First Career Change

I eagerly expect and hope that I will in no way be ashamed, but will have sufficient courage so that now as always Christ will be exalted in my body, whether by life or by death. For to me to live is Christ and to die is gain. (Philippians 1:20–21)

In 1952 when our second daughter, Linda, was born, I was pursuing a career as an electrical engineer and engineering manager in the military electronics field. Within a year of her birth, my wife, Hazel, and I noted her failure to begin speaking as her older sister, Carol, had done at that age. It was not because "she is just a little slower, remember, all children are different," the traditional reaction from the family doctors and grandparents. It was because she was deaf.

Over the next five years, we confirmed the degree of her hearing loss and accepted the fact that there was no surgery or medication that would correct the situation. It was then we began to seek guidance in our daily prayers as to what was God's plan for my family, my career, and me.

At this point in our marriage we had not yet begun to use My Problem Cards, but I vividly remember the circumstances and can easily reconstruct what a My Problem Card would have said.

June 1953: Lord, we have not had any deafness in either of our families. We believe that all things work together for good for those who love You and that You are in complete charge of Linda's life and ours. What does this unexpected situation mean to my career and our family? How can we best help Linda prepare for adulthood and at the same time meet the needs of the whole family? Please, God, we need Your help now as we never have before in our married life.

We started first with what later would be called "home schooling." With assistance from the John Tracy Clinic's Correspondence Course, we were able to help Linda adjust to two body hearing aids. Not everyone at that time agreed that two hearing aids were better than one. We became convinced, however, that a second hearing aid would give Linda more directional hearing such as a person with normal hearing has by virtue of having two ears. After all, God gave everyone two ears for a reason best known to Him and we wanted Linda to have what everyone else had been given.

We helped Linda to begin to acquire the skills that would be necessary for reading, writing, and speech. We wanted her to become an oral deaf adult, which meant she needed to acquire as much as possible those skills needed to function in a hearing and speaking society. At age three, she was enrolled in nearby Mill Neck Manor Lutheran School for Deaf Children, which she attended for two years as a preschool day pupil.

Soon we had another baby, Joyce, whom Linda could learn to love and "mother" as most little girls like to do with a younger sibling. As the family proceeded to mature and face continuing challenges, a persistent question kept arising: "Lord, why did You give us this little girl with a hearing problem?"

By the spring of 1958, many changes had occurred in our lives. We had moved from Long Island to Easton, Pennsylvania, where I had bought into a small, well-established electronics company. I was elected president of Radio City Products, Inc., and for the first time in my career was CEO and chief stockholder of my own company.

Joyce and Linda were both attending Faith Lutheran Elementary School. Carol, our oldest daughter, was attending Middle School in Easton. We arranged for Linda to receive daily private speech and language therapy from Mrs. Helen Beebe, a private therapist in Easton. Mrs. Beebe had an international reputation as a highly talented teacher of speech to congenitally deaf children. She just "happened" to live and practice in Easton, where I now had a new position.

We purchased a comfortable house near Mrs. Beebe's office so Linda could walk safely from our home to her daily lessons after coming home from Faith Lutheran School where she attended classes with normally hearing students. It really looked like things were all in order for expanding my career as an engineering administrator and getting the best possible educational services for Linda and her two sisters.

A question still remained in our thoughts and prayers. What did God really want me to do with my time and talents? Did the appearance of Linda in our family possibly indicate that He had other plans for my career and our family? This thought kept popping up in our family prayers, but it never actually reached the level of challenging me to change my career.

It wasn't long, however, before I realized that all was not well at Radio City Products.

February, 1960: Lord, I am really in trouble. I have learned that the previous owner underbid several government contracts. We are losing money every day we stay in operation. My business partners have no more money to invest to stave off potential bankruptcy and neither do I. I am working day and night to find a legal way to avoid company failure, but it doesn't look good. It certainly looks like my career is going to change dramatically whether I like it or not. Oh, Lord, I trust You implicitly to show me what I should do.

While deeply immersed in my company problems, I still maintained an active interest in working on my family needs at home, especially for Linda. Hazel and I had joined the Alexander Graham Bell Association for the Deaf on the recommendation of Harriet Montague, our parent counselor at the John Tracy Clinic based in California, named for Spencer Tracy's deaf son.

Mrs. Montague had suggested membership in the Bell Association, a nonprofit organization that advocated the teaching of speech and language skills to hearing-impaired children. She said it would be an excellent step toward learning how to be better parents for Linda and her sisters. It would also help us to become acquainted with other parents of deaf children. We joined immediately.

The Bell Association, founded by the inventor of the telephone, held national meetings in a different city every other year. I was elected secretary of the parents section, so I was expected to attend each biennial convention. We had attended several of these meetings and found them to be very helpful. We read the *Volta Review*, the professional journal of the Bell Association, and thereby gained an enormous amount of knowledge as well as many contacts with other parents and professional educators.

By January 1962, it became evident that Radio City Products was about to close down. After much prayer and loss of sleep, I decided to place a classified job wanted ad in the *Volta Review*. I was understandably apprehensive that my lack of professional training in deaf education might make it seem a little foolish for me to be seeking a teaching or administrative position in the field. The next Bell Association national convention was coming up in Detroit in June, and I hoped I would be able to schedule some interviews in response to my ad.

> June 15, 1962: We are on our way today to the Bell Association National Meeting in Detroit. I have not had a single response to my Position Wanted ad in the *Volta Review*. Am I crazy to think anyone would hire a man with no formal training in education and a recent history of being president of a bankrupt electronics company? I had really hoped I might have had a response or two by this time.

We arrived at the Detroit hotel that served as headquarters for the convention and registered. Not long after we settled into our room, I was walking through the lobby greeting friends from across the country when I was approached by the president of the Bell Association, Dr. George Pratt. He asked if I could meet with him in his room as soon as possible. I agreed, not asking the purpose of the meeting, but assuming it had something to do with my role as an officer of the parents section.

Dr. Pratt got to the point immediately: "Our executive director, Mrs. Johnson, just informed me this morning that she is resigning her position in two months so she can accompany her husband to a new work assignment in Europe. I understand you have advertised in the *Volta*

Review for a position in the field. Would you be interested in becoming executive director of the association and moving to Washington?"

I was shocked. I told Dr. Pratt I would give him an answer in the morning after speaking to Hazel and walked out of his room in a daze.

> June 15, 1962: Lord, for months I have been wondering what I should do about my career and my failing business. I have felt that maybe I should open a school for teaching speech and language to deaf children in eastern Pennsylvania, but I have very little training for such a venture. I know quite a bit about managing (and mismanaging) an electronics research and manufacturing company but not much about running a school.
>
> Today in Dr. Pratt's hotel room I experienced the presence of the Holy Spirit in a way I have never done before and may never again. Shivers went up and down my spine as I listened to Dr. Pratt offer me a position that I never dreamed of filling. This is exactly what I know I can do, and You, Lord, have chosen it for me. Never before in my life have I felt the real, live presence of the Holy Spirit as I did today. Guide me, Lord, as we consider this opportunity that You have created.

The salary Dr. Pratt offered was less than one-third of what I had been earning as president of the electronics company. We would have to move from a small city in eastern Pennsylvania to a location in or near the big city of Washington, DC. This would mean selling our home in Pennsylvania and purchasing another near Washington.

Each of the girls would have to be enrolled in a new school. We would have to find a good speech and language therapist for Linda.

I sat in our hotel room that night and wrote a long list of all the commonsense reasons that this would not work. Hazel made her own list. After talking and praying about all the questions, however, it was clear we had no choice. The decision had been made for us by the unique set of circumstances that had opened up. We concluded that there was no position in the whole world that would more ideally meet my deep spiritual needs and make use of my business and electronics experience than this position as executive director of the Alexander Graham Bell Association for the Deaf and editor of the *Volta Review*.

The next day I advised Dr. Pratt that I was ready to move to Washington and begin work as executive director. He offered me an annual salary of $8,000, but after a bit of discussion he generously increased it to $10,000.

We made the change and never regretted it. Over the next sixteen years, we adjusted to the metropolitan Washington area that was, and still is, the capital of the free world. That in itself meant wonderful opportunities to visit famous museums and government buildings, meet politicians, and see the Japanese cherry trees bloom in the spring. It also meant beginning a new job in a different field, new schools for the children, new therapists for Linda, and a host of other adjustments.

My new job involved working with many boards and committees, planning new programs, preparing and delivering testimony relating to new legislation before committees of Congress, addressing professional organizations relating to improved means of educating deaf children, and much more.

As editor of the *Volta Review*, an international publication for professionals and parents, I traveled all over the world to attend meetings of teachers, administrators, and parents. I consulted with commercial companies in the creation and distribution of innovative devices to help hearing-impaired persons be more comfortable and productive. In all of these areas of activity, I had the confidence that I was using my time and skills to improve the education and the future for thousands of children with a hearing disability.

God had indeed provided a solution that I never could have imagined and at just the right time in my life.

It seemed that it all started in that Detroit hotel meeting with Dr. Pratt, but I knew better.

Chapter 2 ∾

Can We Afford
This House?

By faith Abraham, when called to go to a place he would later receive
as his inheritance, obeyed and went, even though he did not know
where he was going. (Hebrews 11:8)

In 1962, we moved from Easton, Pennsylvania, to Silver Spring,
Maryland, a suburb of Washington, DC, where I had taken a new job
as executive director of the Alexander Graham Bell Association for the
Deaf. The salary was less than one-third what I had been receiving at
my previous job in Easton.

We moved from a lovely four-bedroom house in an upscale neighborhood in Easton called College Hill to a small three-bedroom apartment
unit on the first floor of a high rise in the Washington suburbs. That
was all we could afford. It was nice, but it was not where I wanted to
bring up my three daughters for too long.

After about four years there, we began looking around for a house.
We finally found a lovely cape cod for $25,000 that we thought we could
afford. We signed a one-year lease/purchase agreement in the hope that
during that year we could get enough equity out of our old house in
Easton to make a down payment on the new house.

In the excitement of moving from a small apartment to a four-bedroom house with a fenced yard for our dog and near the local schools,

we did not give much attention to the "what if" question: "What if we cannot sell our house in Easton in the next twelve months and get the necessary cash to purchase this new place in Silver Spring?"

December 17, 1966: Lord, today we learned that our landlord will not agree to extend our lease/purchase contract for another year as we have requested. We do not have the necessary cash for a down payment because our house in Easton has not sold yet. We need that money for the down payment on this house that we have been renting.

We have to make some firm decisions by March 1, 1967, as to where we are going to live. I have no idea what is best for us. How will things work out? We will have to leave it in Your hands, Lord. Shall we go back to another small apartment, try to find another house, or what?

Soon we had another problem facing us. The tenants who had been renting our house in Easton moved out and left the place in shambles. In order to make the house more saleable, we decided we had to paint the inside, and we needed to do it immediately. So we began a series of weekend trips to Easton from Silver Spring to work on cleaning and painting the entire house.

The four-hour drives started on Friday night after work and ended late Sunday evening. With help from our three daughters and some of their friends, we scrubbed, painted, and fixed up the Easton house over a period of two months. We knew we needed to make the property more attractive, but it would require a lot of hard labor from everyone.

At first it was fun working together with our three girls and their friends. After a few weeks, however, the novelty wore off and it became a grueling experience. Our joint efforts resulted in a much more attractive house to show to possible purchasers and an opportunity to visit again with old friends at Faith Lutheran Church and our old neighbors in Easton.

February 18, 1967: Our house in Easton is still unsold. Whatever cash we have is tied up in that house. Without cash, we cannot exercise the option-to-buy this house by March 1. Mrs. Herring, our real estate agent in Easton, says our house will surely sell sometime soon, but as of the moment we do not have a buyer with sufficient cash to make a sale. We need a qualified buyer right now. Lord, are you listening?

The deadline was fast approaching. Where would the money come from to make the down payment? We started searching for another small apartment to move into after March 1. Much as we disliked the idea of another move to a temporary location, it appeared that this was the only alternative. We prayed that something would happen, but we did not know what form it might take.

February 27, 1967: Mrs. Herring called us out of the blue today. We hoped she had a buyer, but that was not the reason for her call. She announced that she would loan us the $2100 necessary for the down payment to purchase the Silver Spring house. Lord, we hardly know her. The Fellendorfs are just one of many real estate clients she must have right now. Why is she doing this? This is the last thing we expected

Thank You, Lord, for this very specific answer to our continuing prayers. With this news today, we are able to make the down payment and sign the contract to purchase this $25,000 Cape Cod in Silver Spring. The local bank has agreed to the necessary loan at an attractive rate of 4.5%. What can I say but, "Thank You, Lord"?

We lived comfortably at 1300 Ruppert Road, Silver Spring, Maryland, for the next twenty-one years. Linda and Joyce attended Calvary Lutheran Elementary School. Carol, who was too old for Calvary, attended public schools. They all graduated from public high school and began their post-secondary careers in the Washington area. We had many wonderful neighbors, including Johnny, who became the best friend of our first grandson, Ramin.

We will never forget the pleasant memories associated with that house nor the gracious gesture by a real estate lady we hardly knew that made it all possible.

Chapter 3 ∾

Learning About Childhood Deafness

If you, then, though you are evil, know how to give good gifts to your children, how much more will your father in Heaven give good gifts to those who ask him! (Matthew 7: 9-11)

We love our children, Carol, Linda, and Joyce equally. Each of them has presented us with joys, sorrows, and problems, as can be expected in any family. In our situation, however, Linda called for a special kind of attention that is uncommon among most families.

We detected Linda's hearing loss primarily through parental observation of her behavior in the presence of normal sounds and noises in the home. During the weeks and months preceding the actual medical diagnosis of deafness, we watched and we prayed as we never had before. I can remember creeping into her bedroom and trying to awaken her with a loud clap of my hands. I also experimented with a portable radio turned up as loud as I could make it. But nothing aroused her out of her sleep. Our prayers at that time asked the Lord to help us understand whatever her problem was and to have it corrected. We were totally convinced that whatever it was, prayer and medical attention could cure it.

We eventually had to accept the fact that something was wrong, but one incident sticks in our memory that we will never forget. We were attending a church supper at Carpenter Memorial Methodist Church near our home in Glen Cove, New York. The young children had been placed with babysitters in the church fellowship hall while the adults and older children were attending a rally in the sanctuary upstairs. Midway through the evening, a babysitter came up to me and whispered, "Please come downstairs. Linda is acting very strange."

I rushed to where Linda was standing among a dozen or so other kids. All of them were shouting and playing with each other except Linda. She stood there alone and silent with her eyes closed. I tried to speak to her and held her in my arms, but she kept her eyes closed and would not open her mouth. I feared she was having a seizure so I raced her upstairs and told Hazel we had to leave for home immediately.

As soon as we left the church and hit the cold winter air, Linda opened her eyes and began to act normally. Next morning, we visited our family doctor. We described the events of the previous night at church, and he immediately said, "You better have her hearing checked." He suggested that the night before, Linda might have become distressed with all the commotion in the church fellowship hall and had closed her eyes to remove it from her sight. She was already separated from the sound by her hearing loss. When the cold air in the parking lot announced that she was in a new environment, she opened her eyes and resumed her normal demeanor. A few days later an ear, nose, and throat physician confirmed the diagnosis of our beautiful little thirteen-month-old daughter: "severe deafness."

We never could establish a reason for Linda's hearing loss. Neither of our families had a history of hearing loss, Hazel had not been ill during the pregnancy, and Linda herself had no illnesses that might have caused her to be deaf. But she was deaf. In rather short order, we had to recognize Linda's problem as educational rather than medical. The medical profession had no cure for congenital nerve deafness. There was no surgery, no medication, and no treatment that would restore Linda's hearing.

Our prayer life with respect to Linda focused on her educational, intellectual, spiritual, and social development. How should she be taught to read, write, and communicate? Where should she be taught? Who should have primary responsibility for teaching her?

The My Problem Cards that we began to use when Linda was about six years old reflected our concern for her schooling, her friends, her tutors, and her future. We had no background in handling a little girl with a profound hearing loss, but we rather quickly accepted the fact that she was our little girl, who along with her two sisters, were gifts from God. Whatever it would take to help each one of them mature into competent, self-assured, responsible adults we were obliged to provide.

It would take another volume to report all of the problems and solutions associated with Linda's development into an adult with her own family, home, and job. The My Problem Cards that follow here were selected to illustrate just a few of situations we encountered and how God so richly blessed our family at different points in her development.

January 22, 1967: Apparently Linda failed her math exams and maybe failed in other subjects as well. If these failures discourage her, she may give up and feel overwhelmed. I hope and pray, however, the experience will convince her that she needs to study—intelligently—and that if she does, she can succeed.

A month later Linda got her report card and found she had earned a "C" in math, which pleased her tremendously. She did fail the test, but her grades had been good enough to average out as a "C" for the term.

Her confidence had been shaken, but she was still trying. We thanked God for giving her some hope and perhaps more inspiration to try harder in the future.

May 1, 1967: Today Linda attends her first party with all deaf children. We want her to enjoy herself but not too much! If she gets the idea that all her problems are over when she is in the company of other deaf people, we fear that she will change her outlook and determination. Help us to help her, Lord.

The party was fun, and she did say that she enjoyed being with the other deaf kids. She had a right to be with those with whom she could relax and with whom she communicate comfortably, but we were convinced we must pursue spoken English rather than sign language as her primary mode of communication. This had not yet become the kind of problem that other parents warned us about. We persisted in wanting her to be a part of our world of hearing and speaking people.

August 14, 1967: Please grant Linda a glorious visit to Florida. She will attend a summer workshop at New Smyrna Beach at the summer cottage of Mr.and Mrs. Stibick. May she come back excited, refreshed, and ready to face the problems and the opportunities of her new school, Key Junior High. Help her especially to find new friends who enjoy her and her company.

It was a good trip for Linda. She met boys and girls on the beach, had fun swimming, crabbing, and riding motorbikes. Also, she had plenty of talk with Barbie Bell, a deaf girl her age, that probably included a comparison of problems at home and at school. When she came home she talked for hours about all her experiences and we were so glad she had been able to go.

August 20, 1967: I am concerned about Linda's new school; the teachers, speech therapist, and the counselor, in particular. I hope Mrs. Goldberg, the speech therapist, will be a capable, friendly person whom Linda will like and who will be really effective in helping her with her speech. God grant that she will be that kind of person.

Linda met Sandra Goldberg and said "I love her. She's young, beautiful, and she likes to talk." Also, she seems very interested in Linda. From the way Linda described their visit, she is just the right person.

August 21, 1967: Linda will need at least one exceptionally fine teacher at Key Junior High. Also, with just one sensitive but firm friend, she can make it for another year at Key. Grant that today she will meet her or him. Every girl at her age needs a special confidante and Linda is no exception. Thank You, Lord, for answering this prayer in Your time and in Your way.

September 1, 1967: We met Mr. Ken Twenty, junior high principal, and Mr. Tuner, the counselor. Both seem to be interested in Linda and want to assure her success in junior high. Mrs. Webb is a fine, mature person who will teach Linda's math class. They get along fine, and she has helped greatly in strengthening Linda's self-confidence.

September 15, 1967: Today we meet Mrs. Chaunenet, the new counselor for hearing impaired students at Francis Scott Key Junior High.
I spoke to her on the phone, and she was very interested in Linda.
Grant, Lord, that this woman may be the kind Linda will like, that
she will be quietly constructive in helping Linda through ninth grade
as a *real* member of the class. Grant also, Lord, that this year Linda
may find one or two girls who will be close friends and live near us.
Thank You, Lord.

December 1, 1967: Mrs. Chauvenet has turned out to be a very positive and thoughtful counselor. She is not dramatic but sensible. Her
husband is deaf, which certainly gives her an understanding of Linda's
needs. She has arranged Linda's schedule, met with Mrs. Roblee,
Linda's private speech therapist, and Mrs. Whitehead, Linda's private
language therapist. She talked to all of us for hours on the phone.
Thank You, Lord. The "good friend" is still to come.

December 3, 1967: Linda insists on seeing Eleanor, the one whom
she has picked to be her best friend. I have tried to prevent this by
giving all kinds of excuses, because this girl's parents are deaf, and I
am afraid Linda will pick up their attitudes and mannerisms. I just
don't know if I should let Linda go to Eleanor's house or not...and
I don't know if I can really prevent it anyway.

It was difficult to step back and let the Lord take over at this time.
Certainly we had no animosity toward deaf adults and children. We
were entirely sympathetic to their needs and desires as we were in many
respects in the same situation. But we had committed ourselves years
before to do our utmost to prepare Linda to live in a hearing world
with her family and friends while recognizing that eventually she would
make her own decisions on her own choice of friends, a spouse, and
lifestyle.

January 3, 1968: Linda has pretty well forgotten Eleanor. She still
seeks out more friendships at Key, but she seems to have little need
for Eleanor now. Thank You, Lord.

January 15, 1968: Linda has three or four tests today. She studied, not
well perhaps, but long. Be with her, Lord, and preserve her self-respect

regardless of how she does on these tests. Please don't let her get the idea that she will fail at everything. Thank You, Lord.

Did Linda do well or poorly on her tests? After thirty years, I cannot recall. If I had written it down on the back of the card, I would remember. I do know that Linda had developed by this age a strong feeling of self-confidence that things would work out for her. She was determined, and this made her sometimes difficult to live with. However, this determination was what carried her through some rough times, and so it was a blessing much more than a curse to a teenager with a profound hearing loss.

February 2, 1968: What is the best high school placement for Linda? It looks like a choice between Walt Whitman High School and Sandy Spring Friends School. If the latter is right, we've got to find another $1100 a year. Please lead us, Lord.

I could not find a notation on the back of the card, but we must have found the $1100 somewhere because we did enroll her in Sandy Spring Friends School.

October 18, 1968: Linda is working hard at school. She really seems to be trying, but she is slipping back. Help her, Lord, to keep calm and not give up. Help her with a friend in whom she can confide without pressure. Thank You, Lord.

After dropping Latin, things seem to have improved. She works diligently at her homework, seems confident and happy. Her next marking period will show how well she has really done, but her attitude is good, and that's what's important. Thank You, Lord.

April 4, 1969: Lord, Linda loves Sandy Spring Friends School because she has made friends, but her academic work is still questioned. She is trying more but still finds little to interest her in biology, history, and math. We don't know if we should transfer her to a business course in some other school or fight to keep her at SSFS. Guide us, Lord.

May 9, 1969: I pray that at Sandy Spring Friends School Linda will find real friends and that she will find one or more teachers through whom she can see God's love and God's plans for her life. Linda has made some friends at Sandy Spring Friends School, perhaps more than she has had elsewhere. Among the teachers, however, she seems to have been ignored. Now the school says she has not been doing well, and they are questioning if she should go there for another year. Isn't it strange that at a so-called Christian school, a young lady with a severe hearing loss trying to get an education is ignored by the faculty and administration?

May 28, 1969: Lord, we need help with Linda. We don't know if we expect too much or too little from her. We're confused, worried, and concerned about her future. School placement seems to be our biggest problem, but maybe this is only symbolic of a bigger problem. You know, Lord. Please guide us and Linda to the setting that will restore her self-respect and best help prepare her for adulthood.

June 15, 1969: Lord, it is not just the money for tuition, certainly we could find that if we have to, but she really does not seem to be getting much from the class instruction. The teachers are not cooperating and maybe we shouldn't expect much from them in the way of special help. Each night I listen to audio tapes from her biology class and write down notes for her to study, but I don't really know if it helps. We are trying so hard to help her.

We finally decided to send Linda back to public high school.

We learned enormous lessons over the years as Linda grew through adolescence into adulthood. She became progressively more independent and that certainly was our goal. Of course, there were occasions when we felt she was becoming too independent too fast, and this contributed to family tension. She married Hossein, a young man with a congenital hearing loss, who had come to the USA from Iran to finish his education. They have two sons, Ramin and Kamran, both of whom have a hearing impairment like their parents. The boys are now fine young adults who are married and starting their own families. Linda has held a variety of jobs including one in cosmetics sales with the Mary Kay organization.

March 3, 2003: Lord, today is World Day of Prayer and also the day when Linda, who arrived here in Florida from her home in Mesa, Arizona, last week, will have three Mary Kay cosmetic parties here at Woodlands Lutheran Camp. I ask You, Lord, to watch over her, comfort her, and bless her with Your Holy Spirit. She has real guts to take on several groups of elderly women whom she has never met before and make her presentation. She needs self-confidence and the assurance that You are in control of this new venture on which she has embarked. Thank You, Lord.

March 5, 2003: Thank You, Lord. Linda had three Mary Kay parties, for a total of sixteen women. Her sales were not great, but she made a wonderful impression, and her spirits soared. She felt very confident and satisfied that it was worth the trip from Arizona. Indeed this was an answer to my prayers for this week and this situation. There were no negatives and many positives. I thank and praise You, Lord, for Your answers to my prayers.

Chapter 4

Family Trip to Europe

Then the disciple whom Jesus loved said to Peter, "It is the Lord!" As soon as Simon Peter heard him say, "It is the Lord," he wrapped his outer garment around him (for he had taken it off) and jumped into the water. (John 21: 7)

I grew up in the little village of Sea Cliff on Long Island, New York. My father was a bank teller who often remarked before he died in 1972 how proud and pleased he was to have survived the Great Depression without ever being "on relief." That was the term used in those days for what we call welfare today.

Even though my father had not finished high school, he had always been able to support his wife and three children in what would be referred to as a typical middle-class style. We were a little slower than some of our neighbors in getting our own car and a black and white television, but these were not really that important to our style of living in the 1930s and 40s.

Our family summer vacations focused on visiting relatives in other communities and occasionally going to Polley's Farm in the Catskills. Mr. and Mrs. Polley had a large dairy farm and rented out rooms in the summer. The price was just right for our family. I recall that the room and board for each child was five dollars a week. That was about right for our family budget.

My brother and sister and I were thrilled to get up early and watch the milking of the cows. Then we enjoyed the haying, cleaning the barn, and the other chores so common on a rural farm but so uncommon to residents of a suburban community near New York City.

The thought of traveling to a foreign country where a language other than English was spoken was very remote in our family and in our community. In European countries where twelve hundred-year-old villages were common, a one hundred-year-old village like Sea Cliff, Long Island, would be unusual. As a young boy, I could only dream about gazing up at the towering Matterhorn and what it might be like to have a father who was an Alpine guide. A week at a working dairy farm in the Catskills was what we did for vacation, and we thoroughly enjoyed it.

In 1967, I had been for five years executive director of the Alexander Graham Bell Association for the Deaf, an international organization with members all over the world. That year I was invited to give a speech at an international conference on the education of the deaf in Warsaw, Poland. My employer did not have the resources to send me, and I certainly could not pay for it on my salary.

I felt it was time to place the issue before God Himself for guidance.

> June 8, 1967: I have been invited to give a paper at an international congress on the deaf in Warsaw, where I will be speaking as executive director of the Alexander Graham Bell Association for the Deaf. The association does not have the resources to support my travel expenses, so right now the chances of my accepting this invitation are pretty slim. I would love to take my wife and three young children along too, but I don't have that kind of money.

> Lord, I hope and pray that I can make this summer one that our family will remember with great affection and love throughout our lives. Grant that we may be blessed by the experience of going to Europe, that we may bless others by our presence and witness, and that we may return safely.

I calculated we could borrow some of the money needed for all of us to go to western Europe for two weeks before the congress in Poland began. I cashed in my GI insurance from World War II service, as I considered this exciting adventure with my wife, three children, and my sister, Phyllis, to be more important than death benefits to my family in the distant future. We would fly over together, conduct our family tour, and then the family could fly home while I went on to Poland to deliver my speech. But even with the GI insurance cash we would not have enough money to cover the expenses of the proposed trip.

The Bell Association's board of directors always included at least one member of Dr. Bell's family. Mrs. Lilian Grosvenor Jones, one of Bell's granddaughters, was a member of the board in 1967. She heard of my invitation to go to Poland and speak about her grandfather's lifelong interest in teaching speech to deaf children. In fact, this was his profession before he invented the telephone. Mrs. Jones asked me for the details on the international congress and on our dreams for a family vacation in Europe. Of course, I was pleased to oblige.

June 15, 1967: Mrs. Jones apparently has decided it is important to the Bell Association, to the Bell family members, and to thousands of families with deaf children throughout the world for me to accept the invitation to speak of her grandfather's work at the convention in Warsaw. Without any pressure from me and without any real discussion, Mrs. Jones has advised the board she would contribute one thousand dollars to the association to cover the expected costs of my trip to Europe. Thank You, Lord, for this answer to prayer.

Needless to say, the entire Fellendorf family was delighted to learn that the Bell Association had agreed to accept Mrs. Jones' donation.

We left in early August 1967. We traveled for two weeks in a rented Volkswagen van through the Netherlands, Germany, Austria, Switzerland, France, and Belgium. We sat at the foot of the Matterhorn in Zermatt, Switzerland; we visited Heidelberg, Munich, and the Dachau Concentration Camp Memorial. We walked the streets of Bötzingen along the Rhine River where my grandmother had grown up before coming to the United States as an immigrant. We even identified a distant cousin my father never even knew existed. We traveled along the canals of Amsterdam on a trip that my mother always wished she could have taken.

The sights, the people, the food, the experiences will never be forgotten. Our entire family will never forget this wonderful experience as long as we live. Our children had an experience that I could not in my wildest imagination have ever considered possible when I was their age.

Hazel, my sister, Phyllis, and our girls returned to the US while I flew on alone over the Iron Curtain to Warsaw where my paper at the International Congress of Education of the Deaf was well received. Here I was in an Eastern European country describing how a young immigrant speech therapist in his twenties named Alexander Graham Bell had come to America from Scotland, invented the telephone, and became an independently wealthy entrepreneur. But he devoted much of his time and resources to founding a private organization to help deaf children and their parents all over the world.

I had the feeling that to many of my three hundred listeners at this convention in a Soviet-dominated nation, my description of Dr. Bell's "other career" was a revelation that they had never heard before in their history books or newspapers.

Once again, I experienced a situation in which an apparently insurmountable problem, namely the financial resources necessary for the trip, was favorably resolved when shared with a loving God who already had the solution in hand long before I even asked.

Chapter 5

Earning a Doctorate at Age Forty-Nine

But when God, who set me apart from birth and called me by his grace, was pleased to reveal his Son in me so that I might preach him among the Gentiles, I did not consult any man. (Galatians 1:15)

After I served nine years as executive director of the Alexander Graham Bell Association for the Deaf, the board of directors agreed that it would grant me a sabbatical leave. A sabbatical is defined, and traditionally accepted in institutions of higher learning, as an absence from regular teaching or administrative duties for a year to study, rest, or travel. The implication is that one will be a better professional after having a year off to renew and improve mind, body, and spirit.

"What will I do with a year at full salary to enhance my role as leader of an international organization dedicated to improving the future of deaf children, their parents, and professionals in the field?" That was a question yet to be answered. Since I had no university level degrees in deafness, speech, and hearing, an obvious choice would be to use this year to obtain a degree. I considered other alternatives, but the idea of returning to a university as a student of education rather than engineering made a lot of sense to me and to my board of directors.

As was now my regular practice, I wrote out a My Problem Card and thereby placed the matter in the hands of my Lord.

July 28, 1971: It is 8 A.M., Lord, and the issue before me is: "Should I pursue study toward a doctorate?" Associated with this question is a related one: "Should I address my research and doctoral dissertation to an investigation of what is being done in other countries for deaf children and their parents?"

In the next few days, I will know if the circumstances that are always under Your control, Lord, will lead me toward, or away from, this goal. I have applied to the National Institutes of Health for a research grant to investigate the education of young deaf children abroad and would hope that the grant would cover my travel expenses. Also, I have contacted Teachers College-Columbia University where I am being considered as a candidate for a doctorate degree in education. The response to these inquiries should show me, Lord, the direction I should go for the benefit of Your kingdom, for children with hearing disabilities, my family, and myself.

The negotiations with the National Institutes of Health went nowhere. I did not receive the research grant that I thought might help pay for collecting data in the USA and abroad and doing the necessary research and analysis. It had been a long shot, but I had hoped it might materialize. It did not.

The negotiations with Teachers College at Columbia University, however, were successful, thanks to the support of close friends like Dr. Ann Mulholland and Dr. Leo Connor, who were on the Columbia faculty.

I began to commute every week to New York City by train from Washington, DC, to take classes. My sabbatical would not begin until 1972, but I began taking the necessary courses at Columbia to speed up the acquisition of required class credits for a degree of doctor of education.

September 1, 1971: Lord, it is a busy schedule, but somehow I am surviving. I leave work in Washington early Thursday afternoon and take a train to New York. I take one course Thursday evening before getting a ride to The Lexington School for the Deaf in Queens County where the principal, an old friend, has offered me a free room for the night and breakfast each week. Thank You, Lord, for good friends!

Who would have expected such an accommodation? The answer is "You, Lord."

On Friday I take a total of four classes and leave in the evening on the train back to Washington. The train trips give me lots of time for studying.

The travel, classes, homework, and continuing responsibilities as executive director at the Bell Association were challenging, but God blessed me with good health, determination, and a wonderful wife to back me up. Hazel and I discovered strengths that we didn't know we had. They enabled both of us to survive.

January 5, 1972: I have enrolled at Catholic University in Washington for several courses necessary for my degree at Columbia so I can avoid the time and expense of travel to New York this semester. Thank You, Lord. What a blessing to be able to drive to classes in thirty minutes instead of a three-hour train trip. The instructor in statistics is excellent, and I am gaining a good background that is necessary for my doctoral dissertation on education of very young hearing-impaired children.

My plan now is to travel to Sweden in the fall to collect data on the Swedish program for hearing-impaired children. I haven't yet quite figured how we can finance the travel and living expenses while maintaining our home in Silver Spring for our three daughters. It's in Your hands, Lord.

The program proceeded as planned. Hazel and I lived for five months in the winter of 1972 in Stockholm where Rut Madebrink, another old friend who was a school principal, offered us a free apartment at the Manila School for the Deaf for our entire stay. It was amazing and so refreshing to be offered such gracious help from professional colleagues all over the world.

We worked hard in Sweden collecting data on parent experiences with their young deaf children, including their education and support services. We concluded that the experience of having a child with a disability has many commonalities across the world.

After collecting survey data from parents of deaf children in Sweden, translating the information into English, and visiting a number of schools, professionals, and families, we returned to the US. I began a period of required residency at Teachers College-Columbia University in New York City. I collected similar data from a sampling of families in the United States and began my data analysis.

I lived in a room in a college dormitory in order to be able to concentrate on class work and work on my dissertation. I found, however, that living in a dormitory with much younger students was really frustrating and stressful for a forty-seven-year-old graduate student with a family in another city.

It seemed there was no choice, so decided I had to continue until I got my degree. I had a surprise coming, however, that I had not anticipated.

October 10, 1972: This afternoon I will call on the Kennedy family to which a Swedish teacher had referred me. Gabriella Lidbom had lived with this family in New York to care for their young children many years earlier. She asked me if I would visit the Kennedys to bring them her warm regards from Sweden. I have their address so this is the day for my visit.

I located the Kennedy family on upper Riverside Drive about ten minutes from the Columbia campus and walked over to deliver on my promise to Gabriella to visit them. A uniformed doorman greeted me as I entered the lobby and called up to the Kennedy apartment to announce my arrival. I took the elevator to the tenth floor where I was cordially welcomed. The Kennedys were a lovely older couple who lived in a four-bedroom flat with a balcony overlooking the Hudson River. The balcony gave one a clear view of the George Washington bridge. The Kennedy children had long since married and moved out.

After completing my mission of delivering greetings, I described my academic program, including a description of dormitory living among classmates who were the age of my own children. Mr. Kennedy then made me an amazing offer.

He said they had a home in Spain and would be leaving the next week for the winter season. He asked if I would be willing to move into their flat, water their plants, and be a house sitter until they returned in the spring.

I was stunned. I said "You hardly know me," but they said if I was a friend of Gabriella, I must be OK. It took only a moment more for me to agree to their request and accept their generous offer.

A few days later, I filled a grocery cart with the IBM cards for my dissertation, my books, and my clothes and made the move from the college dorm to the solitude of a four-bedroom flat on upper Riverside Drive with a doorman! I spent the rest of my residency living in this spacious apartment with more than adequate space to work on my computer data, draft my doctoral dissertation, and prepare for my oral examination.

> June 1, 1974: We did it, Lord, You and I together! I have been awarded a Doctor of Education degree from Teachers College-Columbia University. I just received my first letter from my mother addressed to "Dr. George W. Fellendorf." Thank You, Lord, that my Mom was able to share this special event with my family and me.

Hazel and I spent those five fascinating months in Sweden collecting data and observing how a modern socialized country attempts to meet the needs of children with a hearing disability and their parents. It was exciting both professionally and personally.

While we were in Sweden, our daughter, Linda, married Hossein, a young deaf man from Iran, whom we really didn't know that well. Their first child was born about a year after their wedding. I didn't know at the time the full price our family paid for this academic achievement and the trip abroad. I know we would have liked to be home for Linda's wedding and to have supported this young couple with our presence on such an important occasion.

But our presence and support were obviously not in God's plans for us or the newlyweds. In 2006, Hossein and Linda celebrated their thirty-fourth wedding anniversary, so it does seem to have been worthwhile!

Chapter 6

An Unexpected Career Change

Make sure that nobody pays back wrong for wrong, but always try to be kind to each other and to everyone else. Be joyful always; pray continually: give thanks in all circumstances, for this is God's will for you in Jesus Christ. (I Thessalonians 5:15-16)

The Alexander Graham Bell Association had labeled the senior staff member as "executive secretary" since the organization was founded by Dr. Bell in 1890. I joined the association in September 1962 as its first executive director, a change in title that I had requested to make it clear I was to assume more than clerical duties for the association.

I might mention that it was Dr. Bell's granddaughter, Lilian Grosvenor Jones, who initially suggested to me that I insist on a change in job title. She felt it had greater prestige and coincided with the association's plans to move into more of an international leadership position in the field of oral education of children with a hearing loss.

With this kind of initial support and recognition, especially from a member of the Bell family, I felt I had found a career placement that would last until I retired.

November 16, 1977: In this coming week, Lord, I am meeting with the board of directors of the Bell Association. This includes attending a number of committee meetings and personal conferences with board officers. From past experiences over the last fifteen years I feel this week may include some confrontations and disagreements. It goes with the territory! All of these will be true opportunities for expressing Christian love and witness. Please, Lord, may I act so that others will know I am a Christian by my love for them, and let that expression of love be consistent with my responsibilities as executive director.

Only a few weeks earlier the board had unanimously passed a resolution thanking me for my "outstanding leadership performance" over the past fifteen years. In my opinion, and that of many others, I was ideally suited by interest and talent to the position of Executive Director of the Alexander Graham Bell Association for the Deaf. Tensions were beginning to rise, however, with certain board members and staff. The "perfect position" was becoming strained, and there were more and more occasions when I found myself wondering if I could handle the pressure and if this position was still the perfect one for me.

The board finally advised me in early 1978 they were not going to renew my employment contract when it expired in two years. What a shock! After years in the field of special education; building the organization; instituting new services for parents, children, and professionals; earning a doctorate in the field; and speaking out on behalf of deaf children and their parents in professional meetings and parent conferences all over the world and before committees of Congress, I was being told that it was time for me to leave. The only reason appeared to be that some board members thought I was too old at age fifty to fulfill the functions of the office any longer.

May 21, 1978: Lord, I am preparing to change careers again as I did in 1962 when I left the field of engineering management to go into special education. At that time I had absolutely no doubt that my move to Washington was part of Your plan for me, my family, and for the Alexander Graham Bell Association for the Deaf.

Now I face another change but do not have the same feeling of conviction that this is Your plan, because the circumstances of this change seem to be quite different than in 1962. Now I seem to be running away from something rather than going toward something better.

Also, I am uneasy that this time, salary and prestige seem to be so prominent in my motivations.

Lord, strengthen my spirit, my love for You, and my willingness to let You work in my life. May whatever happens take place in a spirit of love, and may others know I am a Christian by my love. Thank You, Lord, for answering this prayer.

My experience in 1962 of being invited by Dr. Pratt to accept this position in that hotel room in Detroit had totally convinced me that God called me to this position for the rest of my professional life. Now I suddenly learned that maybe He had other plans for me of which I was unaware.

June 30, 1978: Lord, it has been a long time from 1962 to 1978, but it seems that my attitude toward the board and the way I have responded to the board's action to terminate my employment contract has made others respect me more as a Christian. Perhaps, in some way, Lord, others will be better able to handle similar situations in their lives by the way I, at least to all appearances, seem to have handled my situation. I hope so. Certainly, at the recent biennial Bell Convention in St. Louis, many people expressed their respect and even amazement at my reaction and response to a board action that many thought to be a "dirty deal" after sixteen years of service.

The board had advised me that my employment contract was not being renewed when it expired in September 1979. I took this action as a clear vote of "no confidence" and immediately announced I was planning to leave on or about September 1, 1978. I did not feel it was appropriate for the association, or me, for me to remain in a leadership position for one more year when the board had clearly indicated it wanted someone else in the position.

My decision to resign immediately meant a pressing search for another position. Several opportunities arose as soon as I announced my plans. The most interesting was an offer to direct a newly-organized non-profit organization, The Hearing Educational Aid and Research Foundation (HEAR).

The HEAR board of directors included John Bordley, M.D., internationally known and respected head of the Otolaryngology Department at Johns Hopkins Hospital in Baltimore, and Dr. Melville Bell Grosvenor, president of the National Geographic Society, another grandchild of Dr. Bell.

> August 6, 1978: Lord, at this point the anticipated EPA contract on noise abatement has not been awarded to the Hearing Educational Aid and Research (HEAR) Foundation where I have been offered job as executive director. There seems to be no sense of urgency on the part of the government to fund this important activity. None of the other job opportunities seem promising. I could well be completely out of work by September 4, 1978, my last day as executive director of the Alexander Graham Bell Association for the Deaf. What do I do if that contract award doesn't come through?

Naturally, I wanted and needed a job, but I hoped that whatever came my way would be more than just a source of funds to pay my bills. I needed to pay my bills, of course, but the new job must be also a source of strength and challenge, giving me an opportunity to use my talents and background in a truly constructive manner. I wanted my departure from the Bell Association to be comfortable too, so that I didn't lose that which I had worked hard to achieve over the years, including the respect, if not the love, of those with whom I have worked.

> October 19, 1978: Lord, You have indeed answered my prayers. The EPA awarded the contract for noise abatement and education to the HEAR Foundation, and I began as its first executive director on October 1, 1978. Thus, I have a job that will pay a decent salary and give me a great deal of personal satisfaction, as it involves prevention of hearing loss from exposure to excessive noise to adults and future generations of children and youth. I thank You and praise You, Lord, for Your response in this fashion to my urgent prayers over the past months.

The HEAR Foundation position lasted for about four years and offered me many opportunities to work with some top professional people with international reputations in the field of medicine, audiology, and speech. We organized conferences, produced literature, and offered guidance to private industry, government, and individuals on noise abatement.

Once again, I had experienced the inspiration of writing my problem on a little white card, placing the card in my personal Bible where I could include it in my daily meditations and prayers, and then waiting expectantly for God's solution.

Chapter 7

Cheshire County Christian Coalition

For everyone who has will be given more, and he will have an abundance. (Matthew 25:29)

In 1993, the Cheshire County New Hampshire Chapter of the Christian Coalition faced a big challenge. I was chairman of the organization primarily because I called the first organizational meeting. That is one way most voluntary organizations get started; someone recognizes a need and calls a few friends to get together to talk about it. Every such group needs a leader to call future meetings and set the agenda, so the first one who speaks out often gets elected. So it was with the Cheshire County chapter in 1993.

The Christian Coalition is an organization created by Rev. Pat Robertson around 1990 to inform and encourage citizens who believed in Jesus Christ as their Lord and Savior to become more actively involved in local, state, and national politics. Representatives of the national office helped each state to organize a state chapter, and then county chapters followed as interest developed

Our group had been meeting for only a few months and was still getting itself organized. We were not yet prepared to take on any big challenges, but all of a sudden an issue came up that was to bring our name and our mission to the attention of the public in Keene, in the entire state of New Hampshire, ultimately to the whole nation via national TV.

A member of the Keene school board announced that she felt it would be healthy and convenient to make condoms available to students in Keene Middle School and Keene High School. This was her suggested way to reduce teen pregnancy in our community. No one really questioned her motives for this proposal, but we did seriously question the approach she proposed.

> May 10, 1993: Tonight is the first public hearing on the proposed condom distribution approach to reducing teen pregnancy and teen promiscuity. The Christian Coalition has informed the public about the meeting and encouraged people to attend and to speak out if they have a position on this idea. We anticipate the media will attend and report the attitudes of people pro and con.

> Are we on the right track, Lord? Is this an issue we should be addressing with this new organization? Are we moving too fast or too slow?

This was my first experience with a public hearing on this subject. As chairman of the local chapter, I was nervous about exposing parents and teens to ridicule for trying to focus public attention on abstinence rather than so-called "safe sex." People were looking to me for leadership and I was not sure I was the right person for the job at this moment.

> May 14, 1993: About thirty-five people showed up at the public hearing. I was impressed, Lord, that we had touched this many who were willing to come out and take a stand. Not too many spoke out, but they all listened intently to the rationale, and after the meeting we discussed it in detail.

The chapter members began to respond through letters to the editor to what they considered an inappropriate move by our locally-elected school board. The situation promised to be the first test of whether the Christian Coalition truly represented a majority of the families with school-aged children in our community.

June 16, 1993: Another public hearing on condom distribution and fifty people came out this time to listen and protest the proposed action. I testified on the legality of the issue and the potential liability of school board members if children became pregnant after being advised to use condoms. I have gotten plenty of good legal advice from national sources on these issues and have shared it with others.

Several people approached me after the meeting ended to ask for more detailed information on the next scheduled hearing and if there was anything they could do to prepare for it. I feel much more comfortable and assured that we are on the right track now that others outside our small circle of friends want to become informed and involved. One couple asked if I was going to run for a position on the school board myself and I answered that I was praying about it.

June 28, 1993: After a thorough discussion at the regular meeting of our chapter today, we began a petition campaign to oppose the distribution of condoms in the Keene public schools. I have said that one thousand signatures is our goal, but that may not be Your goal, Lord. Maybe, like Gideon, we should settle for three hundred and not worry about numbers.

I know You will guide us, Lord, and Your will be done in Your time and in Your own way. I pray for wisdom and patience to wait for You to guide us and not get ahead of You. It is clear, however, that it is the consensus of the Cheshire County Christian Coalition membership that freely distributing condoms to children beginning at ages twelve and thirteen is not the way we want to go.

A total of eight hundred citizens signed our petition against condom distribution! An impressive response, but we were not sure how much it impressed the school board. Our members began to attend school board and committee meetings, public hearings, and related events concerned with condom distribution in the public schools. It wasn't long before our public statements at such meetings and our letters to the editor were earning our members labels that included such terms as right-wing radicals, social conservatives, unrealistic parents, and religious bigots.

We really had little time or inclination to think about anything other than this local issue that had aroused the entire community. At one point, NBC-TV news sent a team to Keene to record the debate on condom distribution and some of us appeared on the nightly news nationwide.

The issue still resided with the school board, who, as our elected representatives to run the school system, had the final decision. The board members reminded us that they had no legal responsibility to listen to or follow the recommendations of local citizens speaking out at a public hearing. We waited with anxious hearts to hear their final decision.

> April 27, 1994: Today, the Keene school board finally voted on a motion to distribute free condoms in the public schools. It was defeated 7-1. The only member who voted for the motion was the same lady who had the idea a year ago. Thank You, Lord, for guiding us in this critical decision, and thank You for the seven school board members who voted to reject the motion.

Thus ended an experience in informing citizens on an issue of vital importance to them and their families and then organizing an informed citizenry on how to express their feelings to elected officials. This was a learning experience for me, and I believe the Lord arranged it for a purpose. We were invigorated and encouraged to speak out on other such issues in the community and eventually achieved a degree of respect from our neighbors and the media, though, as expected, not all agreed with the positions taken by the Cheshire County Christian Coalition Chapter.

Chapter 8

A Host of Challenges, Opportunities, and Decisions

Who shall separate us from the love of Christ? Shall trouble or hardship or persecution or famine or nakedness or danger or sword? As it is written: "For your sake we face death all day long; we are considered as sheep to be slaughtered." No, in all these things we are more than conquerors through him who loved us. For I am convinced that neither death nor life, neither angels nor demons, neither the present nor the future, nor any powers, neither height nor depth, nor anything else in all creation, will be able to separate us from the love of God that is in Christ Jesus our Lord. (Romans 8:35-39)

The My Problem Cards have continued to help me recognize God's hand just about every time I faced an opportunity and the need for a decision in my career. Once you get in the habit of jotting down situations where you feel a need for God's assistance, you find that just about everything in your life qualifies for help from Him. As Hazel and I considered alternative ways to utilize our talents and resources to serve the kingdom, we encountered barriers and decisions. The scripture quoted above helped us to resist the many things that would tend to separate us from the love of God through our Lord and Savior Jesus Christ.

In 1988, we moved to New Hampshire from Silver Spring, Maryland to be closer to two of our three daughters and their children. It was a good move, and eighteen years later we continue to feel quite comfortable in New England.

Of course we had to adjust to the fact we were considered "flatlanders" by our neighbors who had been born and brought up in New England. Over a period of years, however, we gained a degree of acceptance that reflected itself in several short-term paid positions and many opportunities for volunteer work.

I served for three years as a commercial real estate agent for a local firm, which gave me a chance to meet local business leaders in my new community. That turned out to be a nice way to get to know some of the "movers and shakers" in southwestern New Hampshire and our neighboring state of Vermont only fifteen miles away.

I was encouraged to run for political office as one outcome of my real estate experience. I discovered, however, I had not lived in the state for the two years necessary to qualify as a candidate for the state legislature. Hazel was not happy about my seeking an elective office in the first place, so I did not pursue this possibility even after I was able to meet the residency requirement.

Around 1994, I was offered a position as executive director of the Early Intervention of New Hampshire (EIN), and I accepted. EIN is a confederation of local centers that served the needs of young children with disabilities and their parents. The headquarters office was in Concord, New Hampshire, about a one-hour drive from Keene, but I found I could perform many of my required functions from home using the telephone and e-mail. The job brought me into contact with a number of wonderful young children with various disabilities from all over the state, their parents, and their teachers.

At EIN, I created and edited a monthly newsletter, organized training conferences for staff, and addressed parent meetings all over the state. It was a fun job and reminded me of my earlier career with the Alexander Graham Bell Association for the Deaf.

After three years, I retired from my role with EIN. I had become interested in the Christian Coalition and found that such an affiliation did not mix well with the EIN reputation as a nonpolitical service organization. I was almost immediately selected to serve as chairman of the New Hampshire State Christian Coalition.

Three years later, in December 1996, I retired from the Christian Coalition leadership in order to devote more attention to the needs of our church, Trinity Lutheran, in Keene. I joined the fundraising committee and served as an educational and management adviser on the plans for expanding the forty-five-year-old preschool program at Trinity Lutheran Church into an elementary school extending to eighth grade.

We were successful in raising the $1.5 million necessary to build a 14,500 square foot school building and to get started on the expansion of staff and student population to the eighth grade level. When a full-time principal could not be found to take over that position, the school board offered me the job for six months. It lasted for two years!

After two years as the acting principal of Trinity Christian School, a position which I thoroughly enjoyed, I had to plan on "what next."

January 3, 2002: Lord, I am beginning to wonder what do I do with my time and talents after June 30, when I retire from my job as acting principal at Trinity Christian School. What will it be? I am confidant that circumstances will show me exactly what You want me to do. So I live expectantly every day, looking for the circumstances that will show me Your will. Thank You, Lord, for answering this prayer in Your time and in Your way.

We decided to use the school's winter break in 2002 to visit friends in Europe, some of whom we had not seen in a number of years. It was a refreshing experience although busy with experiences that kept us on the move. However, the issue of what to do after June was on my mind and in my prayers. When we finally returned to Vienna to catch our flight home, I had devoted many thoughtful hours to this subject. I had one experience in Vienna, however, that called for special prayers that could not wait until I got home.

May 5, 2002, Vienna, Austria: Lord, I am feeling sorry for myself to-day. After three glorious weeks in Hungary and Austria with Hazel and friends from Europe, I am depressed by a few insults to my integrity and my motivations as a Christian by some of my closest friends.

Lord, show me how I should act and speak in the face of this kind of criticism. I was hurt, deeply hurt, but I must do nothing that will not bring glory to Your name.

By the time we arrived back in the United States, I got over my "miff" and worked at clearing my memory of the incident that caused it. The incident did remind me of how easy it is for us to sometimes make a comment to a good friend and inadvertently threaten an otherwise close relationship.

Back in Keene, the issue of school leadership still had not been resolved.

May 30, 2002: No replacement yet for me as principal of Trinity Christian School and no doors are opening for me. I contacted the Association of Christian Schools International and said I would be interested in short-term consulting with other Christian schools in New England. I will send them a resume and see what happens. I put the issue in Your hands, Lord, and ask for the patience and perception to see Your will for me—at age seventy-seven!

The retirement proceeded as planned and everyone was most gracious. I was especially pleased at the retirement ceremony where the students and teachers presented me with some wonderful letters, poems, and songs. Also, the parents and students purchased and planted on the school grounds a Liberty Elm tree that was dedicated to Hazel and me. There was nothing they could have done that would have pleased me more. The Liberty Elm has a special patriotic meaning, having received the name during the American Revolution. The selection of a Liberty Elm fit most appropriately with my love of my country and my love for the children of our school.

July 4, 2002: I am retired—again! Praise God that I made it in spite of some problems that at one point I thought might cause me to leave the school earlier than June 30. Thank You, Lord, for giving me the strength to complete this assignment that was supposed to be six months but lasted for two years.

There was no replacement for me as principal on the horizon at this time, but I left anyhow. I had advised the board in writing six months earlier that I would not continue into the next school year. I was certain that the Lord would provide an appropriate person to take over leadership before school opened in late August. In fact, a qualified replacement was hired just in time for the first days of classes.

August 14, 2002: Today I read Oswald Chambers' (*My Best for His Highest*) selection for August 14. It said to me that I should be ready for a new challenge. What is that new challenge, Lord? I have my health, a clear mind, and talents in speaking, writing, and organizational planning. What do You want me to do? Thank You, Lord, for answering this prayer.

I explored many possibilities by writing letters and speaking with informed individuals. For several months nothing appeared that would indicate the Lord had opened a door for me. He did, however, close a few doors, and it was perfectly obvious to me that I should continue to pray and look forward expectantly for His direction. My proposal to the Association of Christian Schools International was not accepted.

February 12, 2004: Lord, today, I received a letter signed by the Secretary of Veterans Affairs in Washington, DC, inviting me to accept an appointment to the Veterans Advisory Committee on Education. I sent a note to the White House two years ago expressing an interest in serving the Bush administration as a volunteer in some kind of advisory role. This opening at the VA seems to have been chosen for me, and I will be happy to accept it.

The position involved meeting four times a year with other committee members to review policies and practices of the Veterans Administration with respect to educational opportunities for our nation's veterans. We were charged to explore new approaches and to make annual recommendations to the secretary. I immediately acknowledged the invitation and my acceptance. I welcomed this God-given opportunity to contribute to the welfare of men and women who have served our country and for me to witness to my faith and trust in You, Lord, in this new situation.

My VA appointment lasted until the end of 2005, when I asked that it not be renewed. I found that the committee spent most of the time on plans for securing increased funding for veterans' educational benefits, a matter that took on great importance when members of the National Guard and the Reserves were being called up in large numbers for longer terms than before. The war in Iraq brought different needs in the Montgomery GI Bill of Rights, and I was pleased to be a part of the committee when it succeeded in obtaining the necessary corrections to federal laws and procedures.

I felt that committee membership required knowledge and experience that I could not offer and therefore I asked to be replaced. The Secretary of Veterans Affairs apparently agreed.

> January 1, 2006: Lord, I asked for an opportunity to serve at the national level and it came through, so certainly my prayers appeared to have been answered in Your way and in Your timing. I did not specifically ask for a Veterans Administration appointment, but that is what came and I gave it a two-year best try. As in so many things, however, it did not turn out to be as productive and successful for me as an individual member as I had anticipated. Maybe I should have not accepted the appointment when it was offered and should have awaited another opportunity more appropriate to my background.

To some it might appear that I did a lot of jumping around, but in each of these opportunities I could clearly see God's hand. I have been excited and stimulated each time as I await the circumstances of my situation to show me how I could best use my time and talents to assist others.

Surely the life of our Lord Jesus was an example of a life in service to others with the ultimate service the giving of His own life for all. No such opportunity will ever face an ordinary human being. God will never send another son to earth to die for sinful humanity, but the example of Jesus' life of service and sacrifice can and does provide a model of behavior for each of us to emulate to the best of our ability.

Good Friends Face Illness and Death: Nancy

Now to him who is able to do immeasurably more than all we ask or imagine, according to his power that is at work within us, to him be glory in the church and in Christ Jesus throughout all generations, forever and ever! Amen. (Ephesians 3:20)

Nancy moved on to her heavenly home on March 10, 1999, just one month before her fifty-first birthday. She had been diagnosed with pancreatic cancer seventeen months earlier when I began to write My Problem Cards with her name on them. In spite of an initial prognosis that she would have only three months to live, Nancy asked for prayers and began medical treatment for her condition. In response to her prayer request, a number of her friends joined a twenty-four-hour, seven-days-a-week prayer team. Hazel and I selected 6:00 A.M., which is when our wake-up alarm called us to a new day. Each morning we lifted Nancy and her devoted husband up in prayer, asking God to provide them with strength and courage for the day ahead, and if He willed it, complete recovery from her pancreatic cancer.

October 10, 1996: The diagnosis of cancer in her pancreas and liver has been confirmed. The doctor opened her up, removed her gall bladder, but then closed the incision and said there was no point in going further. He has given her three months to live at the most.

Nancy and her husband have placed their complete faith and trust in the Great Physician. I am confident that this is a wise decision and clearly they agree.

Nancy has a great faith in You, Lord, and her faith sustains mine. I ask You to heal her in a miraculous way, which I know is totally possible, so that she can be a living witness to Your love and power. Thank You, Lord, for answering this prayer in Your own way and in Your own time. Please grant her release from pain and suffering as she struggles to maintain her faith in Your love for her. Her trust in You, Lord, is a blessing to all who know her.

Hazel and I went to visit Nancy and her husband. We prayed with them and let them know that each morning we would bring both of them to the attention of a loving God who had the power to overcome any illness. They welcomed our visit and our prayers but appeared completely confident that God was with them and in charge no matter what the future was.

November 27, 1996: Thanksgiving Day. Nancy has her family, including her brand new granddaughter whom she thought she might never see, with her for the holiday. Praise the Lord! She is thrilled to see the baby and capture for the moment the appearance of a new soul in their family.

I knew that this traditional family day was especially blessed with the presence of a new life to celebrate. I am sure a lot of photographs were taken and some video as well. The family had much for which to be thankful this year.

December 7, 1996: Nancy called to invite us to their annual Christmas party for friends and her husband's co-workers at the hospital. She feels fine. As we left the party I said, "So long until we return from Florida in April." She answered, "I'll be here."

Here was another glorious occasion to share in a traditional way with friends. It was so heartening to open grab bag gifts to exchange them with other guests, to laugh, and to quietly hope that there would be another such event for Nancy and her family next year.

February 9, 1998: Sheri called us at our Florida home to say Nancy is in the hospital and may not survive the night. I called her in the hospital to pray with her. We agreed that we would meet again when we returned to Keene in the spring or at Jesus' feet. I closed the conversation with "good night," not "good-bye." I could assure her we would meet again "in the morning," wherever that might be.

Every week brought different news, some good and some not so good. The constant challenge was to remember that God's hands were able to handle burdens that ours could not. There is a famous spiritual that says, "He's got the whole world in His hands," and that hymn kept surging through my thoughts as I struggled over the question, "What can I do?" I finally realized that there was nothing I could do personally but to keep placing my concern for her spiritual and physical health in God's hands and let Him decide the future.

March 2, 1998: The word from Keene is that Nancy is back in the hospital again with a temperature of 104. She has just had two pints of blood.

Once again there was a sense of crisis that is always particularly frustrating for the nonprofessional who does not understand test results and their meaning for the friends we love. It is not that the doctors are in error, but we are not able to evaluate such information. We put our own interpretation on what we hear, and often it results in our substituting our dreams for what the doctors are trying to tell us.

April 4, 1998: Nancy's pancreas has begun functioning again. Her priest gave her the last rites in January, but she is still here. In fact, I learned today that she and Alex just returned from a four-day vacation in the mountains, where they did some kayaking and mountain climbing. A month ago I would not have imagined this possible. Thank You, Lord.

April 13, 1998: Back from Florida, we attended Nancy's fiftieth birthday party, an event she was told she would never experience. To God be the glory!

For several years, I had been conducting a weekly radio talk show called "Fellendorf & Company" on a local AM broadcast station in Keene. As I came to recognize and appreciate the tremendous faith in a loving God that Nancy was exhibiting for those who knew her condition, I was led to ask her if she would consider being my radio guest at some time. At first she said, "not now," but then one day she called and said, "I think I am ready to be your guest on the radio."

October 17, 1998: Today Nancy will be the guest on Fellendorf & Company, my weekly radio show on station WKBK. Lord, please guide my words and my heart as we try to reach out to thousands of listeners, including people with cancer and their families, to help them to know You and trust You in their concern, pain, and the eventual move on into Your eternal kingdom.

The program was magnificent! I was so proud of Nancy. Her husband joined her in the studio, but she really didn't need him for more than moral support. Her sincere faith and confidence in her God was so evident.

October 18, 1998: Thank You, Lord. In her own quiet dignified way, Nancy expressed her love for You, her family, and for life itself. She thanked You, Lord, for each and every blessed day You are giving her. I just know she touched many hearts today. Thank You, Lord, for Your blessings on Nancy and those to whom she reached out on the program yesterday.

The future appeared to brighten for Nancy. We began to prepare for our annual trip to Florida for the winter season, but we postponed it for several reasons, including our invitation to Nancy and Alex's annual Christmas party.

December 10, 1998: Another wonderful Christmas party at Nancy's home with her family and many friends. Good food, but most of all good fellowship with those with whom she has been counting the days she has left. We talked about more tests. She is afraid the cancer has invaded her liver. Nancy thanks You, God, for the time You have given her. She is ready for whatever You have planned next for her. She announced, "I am again at a crisis point and greatly in need of prayers for healing or confidence and strength to submit myself to God's will for me if it is otherwise."

December 19, 1998: We attended a healing service at St. Bernard's RC Church in Keene at Nancy's invitation. The church was packed. The speaker was a compassionate nun who laid hands on anyone who asked for it. It was inspirational. One could feel the real presence of the Holy Spirit

February 26, 1999: In Florida, I learned from Sheri that Nancy is in the hospital again in great pain. I called her to again bid her "good night." Lord, I ask You to bless her with peace and relief, as it appears she is approaching the end of her ordeal. And thank You, Lord, for the months of time for preparation she has had for this critical time in their family. Not only is she ready, but her family as well seems to feel she is about ready to move on.

We kept in touch with Sheri, who has been such a faithful friend of Nancy. Sheri herself had cancer but appeared to be totally cured. I knew she prayed with Nancy and had shared her own experiences. It was so gratifying that Sheri, an evangelical Protestant, and Nancy, a devout Roman Catholic, had found this bond of friendship through Nancy's illness. I was sure this relationship was pleasing to God too.

March 6, 1999: Nancy is leaving the hospital and going home tomorrow. I told her we would be home from Florida soon and she said, "I hope I will be here when you return."

Nancy died a few days later. Were my prayers for Nancy answered? Yes, absolutely. Her witness to her faith in God to her family and close friends and to a radio audience was overpowering. She counted each day as a special blessing, and I am sure others saw her faith and praised the Lord for His blessings on her and her family. I will never forget her and how God used her seventeen-month experience of living life to its fullest for His glory.

This recollection does not end with Nancy's move to heaven. Not long after, Sheri's cancer returned, and within a year, she had joined Nancy at Jesus' feet. What a joyful reunion that must have been!

Heaven will be a more pleasant place because Nancy and Sheri are both there. I will look forward to meeting them again.

Chapter 10 ❧

Good Friends Face Illness and Death: Norm

Blessed is the man who perseveres under trial because when he has stood the test, he will receive the crown of life that God has promised to those who love Him. (James 1:12)

Most adults have experienced the uncomfortable, and sometimes devastating, experience of seeing a relative or close friend diagnosed with a life-threatening illness. I have had that experience more than once. Though it is never an experience that I welcome and surely wish could be avoided if at all possible, I have found the My Problem Card has offered me a constructive approach to handling the ups and downs of a seriously ill person whom I have grown to know and love as a Christian brother or sister.

Actually, death is the ultimate solution to all of man's problems. If we believe in the promise of eternal life earned for us by the death and resurrection of Jesus Christ, we can be assured that our own death will be but a transition from an infinitesimally brief life here on earth with all its problems, illnesses, and pain, to eternal life in a place called heaven, which is free of all problems, including illness, disabilities, pain, and sorrow. The issue for all humans is how we handle the passage through this life on earth to the eternal peace of heaven.

Good Friends Face Illness and Death: Norm

What follows is my experience with a close friend and how he handled a critical phase in his life with dignity, faith, and in anticipation of the fulfillment of all of the promises of God to His children.

At Woodlands Lutheran Camp in Florida, where we had a winter home for twelve years, we found many friends of our own generation who inspired us with their devotion to the Lord and their lifetime of service to furthering the kingdom of God. One in particular was Norm, a retired college professor, high school principal, and in his early years, a classroom teacher of elementary and high school students in Christian schools.

Norm taught an adult Bible class at Woodlands for several years and shared his vision of the future as the Lord had revealed it to him in over sixty years of marriage and guiding young people toward careers of service both in the church and in secular areas.

In late 2002, Norm discovered he had health problems that were not going to go away.

February 2, 2003: Lord, my brother in Christ, Norm, goes today for yet another blood transfusion. I raise him up to You, Lord, and earnestly seek Your will to bring him a marvelous cure of his blood disease. Grant that Your will for him will be many more years of service to You, teaching, witnessing, and praising You. But Your will, not mine, be done. Thank You, Lord, for answering this prayer.

Norm had a number of blood tests and consultations with a variety of doctors and specialists that he shared with me in private conversations. I learned more than I ever really thought I needed or even wanted to know about blood counts, transfusions, and the effects of an imbalance within the blood system of the human body. I almost came to feel I was experiencing what he was experiencing, and I didn't find it comfortable.

February 6, 2003: After his most recent transfusion, which lasted eight hours, Norm's blood count rose from seven to nine. He says it is encouraging. Thank You, Lord.

Norm did not seem to want others at the campground to know how sick he was. He decided not to accept my suggestion that the elders of the church at Woodlands come to his home to pray and lay hands upon him. He firmly believed he was in God's hands and really did not want extra attention or sympathy. He had supreme confidence in God's control of his life. I prayed that God would treat him gently.

February 22, 2003: Norm went in today for another four pints of blood. He was taken by ambulance in the middle of the night. Apparently this cannot go on indefinitely. What is his future? It is entirely in Your hands, Lord, and Norm knows this. He trusts You with all his heart and soul. Thank You, Lord, for his faith in You. It inspires me!

A few days later Norm came to our house to tell me about his recent bone marrow biopsy. He did not know the results yet, but he was not optimistic. His doctor said that in her opinion, at best he had possibly twelve months to live and he needs dialysis and chemotherapy. However, she said she would not do so if she were the patient. He is pondering his quality of life if he chooses to accept or reject dialysis or chemo. Help me, Lord, to be whatever kind of a friend he needs at this critical hour in his life. Thank You, Lord, for answering this prayer.

March 15, 2003: Norm has had unpromising test results and will fly home tomorrow to Illinois to live or to die. Today, he goes again for yet another blood transfusion. He will then fly home to be under the care of his regular doctor. Their son will fly here and drive home with Ginny in their car.

Lord, give me the strength and whatever is necessary to say "good night" to this man of God who has given so much already to further Your kingdom.

On March 30, 2003, we called Norm's home and learned that Norm was in intensive care. The most recent blood transfusion did not result in the boost that it had in the past. I asked God to grant him peace and safe passage.

April 4, 2003: Word has come via another Woodlands family that my friend's body is closing down. He has pneumonia, his kidneys have failed, and other bodily functions are not functioning normally. It would seem, Lord, that without a miracle, Norm will soon be arriving at the gates of heaven and begin to receive the answers to all the questions he has asked over a lifetime of studying Your Word and worshiping Your Son. May You make his journey home peaceful and glorious.

It was timely to pray that God would act in the best interests of our brother, Norm. We had been preparing for the day when we would say "Thy will be done" and set aside any assumptions that we knew better than our heavenly Father what was in the best interests of Norm, his loving wife, and their children. We knew without question that all things are possible with God, but we also knew He would select what was best at this time.

April 5, 2003: This morning I called Ginny at their home in Illinois. She said that Norm had moved on to his heavenly home last night. So he has moved on, Lord, to be with You and the host of saints and angels in heaven. Praise God, he is relieved of the blood transfusions and the prospects of dialysis week after week. What a wonderful witness Norm has been for You, Lord, over his life span of some eighty years. Thank You for enabling him and Ginny to celebrate their sixtieth wedding anniversary here at Woodlands with family and a host of friends.

Thank You that Norm was able to attend the Veterans of the Cross retreat here in Florida just a few weeks ago where we saw him meeting and greeting old friends from all over the nation. To God be the glory, great things He has done. Now he is on his way to his next adventure.

Were our prayers for Norm answered? Of course. When good friends become ill, the immediate tendency is to begin praying for complete recovery. If those prayers are answered exactly the way we requested, we tend to feel we have confirmed the very existence of God and His willingness to answer our prayers. If our prayers are not answered as we prayed, we often turn away with a feeling of failure on our part and an uneasy feeling that God was unfeeling, uncaring, and maybe even unable to cure.

In Norm's case, he understood who was in control of his life and was prepared to accept the answers to his prayers. Praise God for his faith and witness to that faith.

Chapter 11

Good Friends Face Illness and Death: Jack

We know that in all things God works for the good of those who love him, who are called according to his purpose. (Romans 8:28)

Let those who suffer according to the will of God commit their souls to Him in doing good. (1 Peter 4:19)

Jack was a good Christian friend who had transformed a hobby into a dramatic and very professional one-man presentation on the life and contributions of William Tyndale. I first met Jack when we attended one of his presentations at a Christian camp near our home in Keene, New Hampshire. Jack had acting training and experience, so while his regular job was as a paraprofessional at a local hospital, he was very capable of presenting the life, motivations, and contributions of William Tyndale on stage.

I must confess that I knew of William Tyndale only as one of the first to translate the Holy Bible into English. After witnessing Jack's portrayal of the Englishman who was burned at the stake for daring to put the Holy Scriptures in the language of the English ploughman, I became fascinated with the man, William Tyndale, and with Jack, the neighbor who introduced me to the real William Tyndale.

About two years ago after we first met Jack, he became ill and began a series of tests to find out what might be the cause. The My Problem

Cards reflect on the issues and events that entered his life and which initiated my brotherly concern for his future and that of William Tyndale's memory as he was portraying it.

> May 3, 2003: I keep praying for Jack who has now been diagnosed with pancreatic cancer. Oswald Chambers's reading for today in *My Utmost for His Highest* reminds me that perhaps I have been praying out of sympathy for Jack, whom God is gradually lifting up to a totally different level in direct answer to our prayers. It's hard to understand, Lord. Help me in my unbelief.

On a weekly basis we received updates on Jack's condition over the Internet. It was pretty much common knowledge that once one is diagnosed with pancreatic cancer, one might have three or four months to live. Jack was forced to cancel William Tyndale appearances all over the country where he had been scheduled to appear. Lots of friends were praying that the God whom Jack knew and loved so much would reach down with a miracle, but the medical facts were not encouraging.

I sent an e-mail to Jack to mention something that never came up in our conversations in the past. I heard via a mutual friend that his doctor was considering removing Jack's large intestine. I wanted Jack to know that nineteen years ago, my large intestine had been totally removed, and I wanted to assure him that life could go on if this procedure was being considered for him. I hoped that mentioning this personal experience of mine would serve to strengthen him and his family.

> August 29, 2003: I called today and talked to Lynne. Jack had to go back to the hospital today to get his "pump" adjusted. She says he is not doing too well today. No further talk about a colonoscopy.

It seemed that every few days we got an update on Jack's changing condition. Some days it looked encouraging only to be followed by days of discouraging news. As much as we, his friends, were concerned and sometimes confused, we could only imagine how this was affecting him, his wife, and children.

September 11, 2003: Jack today sent an e-mail to say the cancer has now reached his liver and he feels he is losing the battle. He will meet with his doctors next week to see how long he has to live. His faith is strong, but his body is weak. Bless him, Lord, with faith, courage, and less pain in the days ahead.

Our prayers continued in spite of the discouraging news. He was already past the few months usually allowed to a pancreatic cancer victim, so we could praise God that he was still with us at all. Jack even began talking about rescheduling some of his canceled appearances as William Tyndale, and his friends considered this a positive psychological sign.

October 2, 2003: Jack states in an e-mail his doctor now says his liver has not been affected. The diagnosis has changed. Praise to You, Lord, the Great Physician. May Jack fully recover and resume his life with his family, his church, and his portrayals of William Tyndale across the nation.

Jack was quite weak from the massive doses of chemotherapy that kept him in bed most of the time. He had many visitors, but he longed to get out of the house even if only for short trips. Many friends were willing to drive him anywhere he wanted to go, but usually he did not feel up to it.

November 5, 2003: I had an opportunity today to meet Jack face to face after a year of only e-mail and phone contacts. Hazel and I picked him up at his home in Vermont and drove him to a prayer and praise meeting at a private home in Keene. After the meeting, I suggested a visit to the Cheshire Medical Center where Jack had worked for many years, and he eagerly accepted the suggestion.

It turned out to be a wonderful experience for Jack and for me too. We had coffee in the hospital cafeteria where he met many of his old friends and colleagues. We prayed together before I dropped him off at his home, praising God for an exciting afternoon.

That trip to Keene was significant. Jack said that if we had driven right home after the prayer and praise session, he would have gone right to bed and slept the rest of the day. But when he had something to do and felt up to it, his whole attitude changed. The chance to meet old colleagues at the clinic was the best medicine he had had in some time.

November 11, 2003: In an e-mail, Jack now reports that new tests show the tumor has stopped growing and is not invading any other organs. He is delighted and praising God for His mercies. Thank You, Lord Jesus, for this remarkable report that I am sure Jack attributes to prayer and trust. Indeed this is a witness that will challenge all the doubters of Your love and power.

Here Jack was experiencing a change in his condition that I had never expected to see even though I had been praying for it. How often are we surprised when God responds to our prayers in exactly the way in which we had hoped. And how often do we attribute such a recovery to the medical profession whose efforts may have been minute compared to God's intervention. All we knew was that Jack's progress seemed to be amazing and confounding his medical advisers.

November 16, 2003: Gary reports that Jack drove himself from Putney to Keene for this week's prayer and praise meeting. Praise the Lord! Who would have dreamed he would be doing this only a few weeks ago? Obviously, You did, Lord!

Thank You, Lord, that You are giving Jack more time here on earth to further Your kingdom. His witness to his faith in You and his experiences are a clear challenge and a blessing to all of us who know him. You are answering our prayers. Thank You, Jesus.

As we do every year, we took off for our Florida home but kept in touch with Jack by e-mail and telephone. I particularly enjoyed hearing Jack's voice and in the back of my mind kept looking for news that he might begin his presentations again.

December 5, 2003: I called Jack from Florida. His voice sounded weak, but his spirits were up. He needs to restore his voice to its earlier quality and feel comfortable to speak his lines for the hour-and-a-half William Tyndale presentation before he can resume his engagements.

I told him we were praying for him daily and had great expectations for his complete recovery.

December 24, 2003: I called Jack again from Florida to wish him and his family God's blessing on the eve of our Savior's birthday. His voice remains weak, and it worries him. He is so anxious to resume his presentations. I suggested a speech therapist or voice coach to retrain his voice, and he replied he already had made an appointment with an ear, nose, and throat physician on January 20 to discuss exactly this approach.

Over the next twelve months, Jack's voice strengthened and his general strength renewed to the point he could begin with his William Tyndale performances again. We drove to Jaffrey, New Hampshire, to attend his performance along with a number of others from our church in Keene. As I watched Jack perform the role of William Tyndale, who had faced death at the stake for his "crime" of translating the Bible into the English language, I realized I was witnessing a modern-day miracle. All medical wisdom had predicted that by this time Jack would have moved on to be with his Lord, but there he was, playing the part of a Christian martyr before an auditorium filled with children, youth, and adults. Many in the audience did not recognize the miracle they were witnessing that night before their very eyes, but I did.

August 7, 2005: Today came the message over the Internet that I hoped I would never receive. Jack announced to his Christian brothers and sisters that the cancer had returned, had metastasized to his spine and intestines, and his doctors were unanimous that he had but a few months to live.

In preparation for what he now had to accept as a fact, Jack began to do special things with his children, especially the younger boys. One was a visit to museums in Boston. Another was to spend a day at the Plymouth Plantation, a restoration of the first British settlement in New England. He seemed determined to stock up memories for his children to help sustain them for what was on the horizon.

Jack moved on to his heavenly home on February 7, 2006 while we were in Florida. We were unable to attend his funeral services, but we knew where Jack was at the time. I was certain that one of his first contacts in heaven would be William Tyndale. For that I can rejoice and praise God for the gift of His Son in whom Jack believed with all his heart and soul.

My prayers for Jack were finally answered in God's way and in His time.

Chapter 12

A Troubled Student

His mother said to the servants, "Do whatever he tells you." (John 2:5)

As acting principal at our local Christian school, I occasionally was faced with a situation that I really had no professional experience in handling. I had been recruited to serve as acting principal when the previous principal said she wanted to go back into the classroom and just teach. When the school board could not find a qualified person to replace her, they looked at the backgrounds of congregation members and found one with the initials "Ed.D." (Doctor of Education) after his name. That is how they found me.

We reached an agreement that I would serve for six months and, hopefully, someone with better qualifications would turn up to take over. It was interesting, challenging, and fun. I especially enjoyed the contact with the students, who ranged from preschoolers to fourth graders. My principal responsibilities included "lunch with the principal" one day a week, when I had a brown bag lunch in my office with a different couple of students selected by a classroom teacher. They also included disciplining when the teacher needed help and had to send a student "to the principal's office."

May 15, 2002: Today, the fifth-grade teacher and the music teacher both reported to me that a student was refusing to go to music class with his classmates. He is disruptive in class and becoming a real pain to everyone in the school. I have been asked to speak to him.

I immediately called Mike into my office, and we had something of a conversation. I am not sure I made any kind of an impression on him.

He says the teachers make up stories about him, his father has cut his allowance, and his mother won't let him use his computer. Now I know at least some of his problems.

Lord, guide me in how to resolve this young man's problems and restore his relationships with his teachers, classmates, and possibly his parents.

The problems did not go away for Mike. I had the strong feeling that he needed a different kind of stimulation, and I pondered what I could do. I knew I could not change any problems he might be experiencing at home, but I did feel a strong responsibility to do what we could for him during his time in our school. The question was: "What can I do?"

May 29, 2002: Mike came back again with his fifth-grade teacher. She reports all he wants to do is read and will not do his spelling assignments. He tells me he enjoys making model airplanes and he loves to read (*20,000 Leagues under the Sea* for the second time). He is bored with his present school experience.

What do I do for Mike, Lord? Obviously he is operating at a different level than his classmates, and his teachers cannot meet his needs for challenge while meeting the needs of the majority of his classmates.

Mike represented a real challenge for me as school principal and for the school situation in which his parents had chosen to place him. Our small private school of some ninety students did not have the luxury of a school psychologist as would be found in a public school, yet we had a student who needed that kind of professional help.

A Troubled Student

June 2, 2002: Today, after discussing the situation with Hazel, we decided to invite Mike to our home for a weekend. We will ask him to come on Saturday morning and stay until after church on Sunday. Grant us, Lord, an extra measure of your Holy Spirit as we try to get a better handle on this boy's unmet needs and come up with some positive suggestions for his parents, teachers, and classmates.

As principal of a Christian school, I felt this was an appropriate and Christ-like approach. His parents were willing to give it a try, and Mike was at least mildly interested in spending a weekend at his principal's home. It was worth a try.

June 15, 2002: This Saturday morning is a workday at our private school. Mike's dad brought him to school at 9 A.M., and he worked all morning with other students and their fathers pulling stones from the playground and athletic field in preparation for topsoil and grass planting.

In the afternoon, he came with us to our house to help us dig holes and put plants in our garden. Mike seemed to enjoy being with classmates in a non-classroom situation and the manual labor at school and our home.

In the evening, we all went to a Keene Swamp Bats baseball game at the high school ballpark. We had hot dogs and soda for supper. He saw friends from school at the game and seemed to thoroughly enjoy the game and the fellowship. He was no problem at all.

Next morning we all went to Sunday school and church. The school students sang in front of the church and he participated.

I never had to see Mike in my office again after that weekend. His teachers reported that he seemed more relaxed and willing to participate in the classroom. I really had no idea if anything we did on this weekend changed his behavior, but it did change. As so often happens, the Holy Spirit seems to have entered into the picture in response to fervent prayers of those who loved and respected Mike. He was still interested in reading at a level far above his classmates, and he still evidenced boredom with classroom routines at times. He was more respectful of others, however, and perhaps was also more pleased with himself after our weekend of work and baseball.

When dealing with young children, whether yours or someone else's, adults are continually faced with challenges. A child refuses to accept adult direction, which is clearly appropriate and often necessary for his physical and social health. I have often said about my own children when they were small that I wanted them to become independent but not so soon. The solution is often found, with God's help, by putting yourself in the child's place to try to understand the needs he is trying to express at the moment. Then create an environment in which those needs can be met while maintaining the God-given responsibilities we have as parents and teachers.

Family Health

What does the scripture say? "Abraham believed God, and it was credited to him as righteousness." (Romans 4: 3)

In the sixty years since we were married, had three daughters and six grandchildren, the dreadful "C" word had entered in any of our immediate family health files only once. That was for a small melanoma on my neck that in 2002 was quickly diagnosed as cancerous and removed successfully.

Then Carol, our oldest daughter, brought us face to face with cancer in a much more serious manner. Carol's experience with breast cancer alerted us to the fact that probably no family can count on going through life without an encounter with cancer. While Carol had a successful mastectomy and the prognosis is very good, all of our family is now more sensitive to the potential threat of cancer. Sometimes we may have appeared to be overly anxious, but one never knows when or where it might pop up. It just appears wise to be cautious and approach every situation with prayer and a special measure of support from the Holy Spirit.

August 15, 2003: Hazel noticed what she called a "boil" on my chest under my left breast. It seemed full of pus. I tried to treat it with Gold Bond Medicated Powder that dried it up a little but didn't remove it.

With the background of Carol's experience and after praying about what to do, I made an appointment today with the dermatologist at Dartmouth Hitchcock Medical Clinic in Keene. Lord, give me the courage and strength to seek and find Your will in whatever evolves next week.

While awaiting the date of my appointment, I found myself wondering if I was overly anxious. After all, it was only a small thing on my chest, and maybe I was making a mountain out of a molehill.

Americans are known worldwide as a nation of worriers who overwork their medical system with small problems. The question for me was, "Is this a mountain or a molehill?"

Several times I found myself prompted to call off the appointment and just "see what happens." My good wife directed me to keep the appointment and I followed her advice.

August 27, 2003: Today, the dermatologist examined me and says it looked benign, but she could not be sure without a biopsy. She says I will hear back in two to three weeks. In a few weeks, therefore, I will know if it is malignant or not. In the meantime, Lord, it is in Your hands, which are much bigger than mine. I have never had cancer other than that small melanoma on my neck that was successfully removed.

What now, Lord? At age seventy-seven will I be having my first serious experience with cancer and what will follow?

The weeks in between were not easy. When one thinks of all the possibilities that might evolve from a small lesion on the chest, one can get very nervous. But worry is really an insult to God the Father. He says He will do the worrying and He will determine the results. So our role is to trust in Him and go on with our lives in complete confidence in His love and power.

September 9, 2003: The dermatologist called to say the biopsy showed it was a ruptured cyst and negative for cancer. Thank You, Lord! What good news.

The doctor and I then continued on a conversation that began during my office visit. Her family name was obviously of German origin, and so is mine, so our conversation turned to our German heritage. She had referred me to a book entitled *The Ominous Parallel* by Leonard Peikoff that explains how Hitler captured the minds and loyalty of the German people in the 1920s and '30s.

I told her that I had taken her suggestion and had gotten the book at the local college library. She has said she would like to see two video-tapes I have on the life and death of Dietrich Bonhoeffer, the German pastor who was executed in a concentration camp shortly before the war ended. I agreed that I would loan them to her, which she seemed to appreciate.

So maybe this event that started out with a lesion on my chest has led to a new Christian friend. Thank You, Lord, for all Your blessings in this recent period of my life.

This was as close as I ever wanted to get to cancer, but it seems the Lord had some further trials for me.

January 5, 2004: Lord, I have a health problem and need your help and guidance. I have a sore on the base of my tongue that has bothered me for several months. I had a tooth extracted recently and it may be associated with that. At noon today I go to the dentist who extracted the tooth to see what is the trouble. His nurse said it might involve a biopsy, which scares me. Bless me, Lord, with patience and courage for whatever evolves from this visit. Thank You, Lord, for answering this prayer.

We once had a neighbor who had cancer of the mouth and eventually had to have her tongue removed. I will never forget her pathetic efforts to make herself understood when she could not manipulate her speech without a tongue. Visions of that long ago friend haunted me as I drove to the dentist for a diagnosis of my problem.

January 15, 2004: Thank You, God! Dr. Manning found a tiny fragment of bone that he had missed when making the earlier extraction. He quickly removed it with tweezers and a pointed instrument. He said it was lacerating my tongue and gum. No biopsy was required.

He took an x-ray to confirm his opinion, gave me an antiseptic to put on the gum, and sent me home, a very relieved man. Praise God from whom all blessings flow.

Our children grew up, started their own families, and assumed all kinds of adult responsibilities, but they are still our little girls. Anytime they have problems we want them to feel comfortable in coming back and asking for help from their mom and dad.

July 16, 2004: Today I got an e-mail from Linda reporting she could not sleep last night because of unbearable pain in her chest area. She said it is under her left breast and wants to know what she should do. She says she has a doctor's appointment for a week from today but doesn't know if she should wait until then to seek medical help. She wants advice from her mother.

We welcome any inquiry from one of our daughters and count it a blessing that we are still close enough to each of them that they feel comfortable in bringing us into their confidence. We praise God that it is so.

Hazel is sending her a message right now to get to the emergency room at the local hospital in Mesa. Lord, bless Linda with courage and faith in You as she proceeds today. If it is your will, grant her complete recovery from whatever is bothering her and relief from the pain she is experiencing. With her own deafness, a deaf-and-blind husband, and two deaf sons, she does not need any more problems in her life right now!

With the blessings of e-mail, especially instant messaging, which we use all the time in view of Linda's profound hearing loss, we are able to communicate and give her instant advice when we are asked. Many years ago, we had to use the teletypewriter to contact her, but now we can use instant messaging at no cost and much greater convenience. Miracles do happen all the time!

July 18, 2004: I just called Linda about 9 P.M. our time and got her report from her visit to the emergency room. After many tests, the doctors concluded that she did not have angina or a heart attack, which is what we feared. It appears to be a pulled muscle in her chest area. They gave her some pain pills and said she should see her regular family doctor next week.

Thank You, Lord, for answering our prayers in this fashion; no breast cancer, no heart attack, and a pulled muscle that responded to pain pills and recovery after rest.

I thank and praise You, Lord, for Your mercy to our little girl at this special time in her life. She may be fifty-two years old, but she is still our little girl. I had visions of Hazel and/or me flying to Arizona to be with her and care for Hossein while she was in the hospital.

Instead, the news is that their swimming pool has finally been completed, and this weekend they will be enjoying it for the first time. To God be the glory, great things He has done. Amen and Amen.

At age eighty-one, it is not unusual for even a normally healthy individual to begin to have aches and pains that are inconvenient and often downright painful. Hazel's father used to say before he moved on to his heavenly home at age ninety-three: "Old age does not come alone." Now I know more than ever what he meant.

In mid-August 2005, Hazel began to experience sciatic pain in her right leg that started in her hip and moved down the calf of her leg. It became so painful that it began to impact our lifestyle, including canceling dinner parties planned for friends and even missing our weekly Sunday school classes and worship services at Trinity Lutheran Church because she was so uncomfortable sitting or standing for very long.

August 15, 2005: Lord, the pain in Hazel's right leg has been diagnosed as a sciatic nerve problem. She can't sleep comfortably and is pretty miserable. Bless her with relief of her pain and let her get a good night's rest. Thank You, Lord, for answering this prayer in Your time and in Your way.

Hazel had x-rays and our family doctor prescribed pain pills, but they brought little relief. Ten days later, the pain persisted. She began seeing a chiropractor, and this did not bring much relief either. The question, arose, "How long will this go on?"

August 25, 2005: Her pain and discomfort persist. How long must she wait until she can sleep all night and move around with comfort during the day? Friends and family are praying for her, but we do not really know of other things to try.

August 26, 2005: Lord, I decided today to look for other solutions to Hazel's problem. I asked her if I could contact an acupuncturist in Keene and see if we could get an appointment. She agreed, though neither of us had any previous experience with this procedure.

We visited a local acupuncturist, a Chinese medical doctor who came to the United States about twenty years ago after being ousted by the new Communist regime. He asked the type of questions one would expect from a former surgeon and then proceeded to insert six tiny needles in Hazel's back. He attached electrodes and applied a pulsating current as she lay there and listened to delightful Chinese music on his tape recorder.

After thirty minutes, the needles were removed and she rose from the table with a smile on her face. The sciatic pain was dramatically less, and she could walk with ease for the first time in weeks.

September 2, 2005: Thank You, Lord! Today Hazel experienced great relief, and we are so pleased at the success of the acupuncture treatment. Another treatment in a few days is indicated so we will go back next week.

In the intervening period I saw Hazel getting more sleep at night and much greater mobility during the day. She went to our usual Bible class on Sunday and was able to sit through the worship service with no discomfort.

September 6, 2005: Hazel had another treatment today for some lingering discomfort in her right knee. It worked as well as the treatment last week so this has turned out to be a modern miracle. We just thank and praise You, Lord, that You led us to consider acupuncture, a procedure that in the past we would have thought of as a "gimmick." Now we are convinced that at least for this type of hip and leg pain, it is the right treatment. If the situation occurs again, I am sure we will consider acupuncture as the first approach to get relief.

God works through people to accomplish His solutions for our problems, so it makes sense to look for help from professionals and even friends who have had experiences from which we can benefit. Each situation should be brought to God's attention through prayers, and He will guide us who to accept and when.

Chapter 14

Serving God's Children in Slovakia

He will call upon me and I will answer him; I will be with him in trouble, I will deliver him and honor him. (Psalm 91:15)

As you exit from our church parking lot in Keene, NH, there is a sign that says, "You are now entering the mission field." It reminds us that we do not have to travel to darkest Africa or to a remote island in the South Pacific to find people who have not heard of Jesus Christ, or if they have, have not accepted Him as their personal Lord and Savior. The sign encourages every member of our congregation and every visitor as well to be alert to mission opportunities in one's family, neighborhood, office, and social contacts. Each believer has a call to reach out to someone, somewhere with the gospel message.

With that thought in mind, and having listened to missionaries who have spent years in Thailand and Russia bringing the gospel message to those who have never heard it in any language including their own, I prayed about finding an opportunity where my own special talents, experiences, and background might be ideally suited to furthering God's kingdom. I debated with God and myself whether He wanted me at age eighty to go abroad or simply to devote my remaining years to witnessing in my own community.

April 14, 2004: I awoke early this morning and prayed again for guidance on how to spend my skills, experience, and faith in my years to come. I have registered my interest in missionary work with Trans World Radio, an international organization that broadcasts by AM and FM radio the Good News of Jesus Christ in 190 different languages and dialects.

I have also contacted the Lutheran Church-Missouri Synod for a list of areas where missionaries are needed throughout the world. Maybe I don't need a missionary assignment away from my home and family to fulfill my desire to serve the kingdom. I just want to use my life and talents to be an effective witness to You, Lord. Will You guide me, please?

It seems to be difficult to ask for help and then have the patience to await the circumstances that will reveal God's answer. I found a long time ago I was no different than any other impatient man in today's society. We pray and ask and then expect immediate and clear answers to prayer.

May 12, 2004: Yesterday I had a call from the missionary board of the Lutheran Church-Missouri Synod, asking me if I would be interested in a volunteer missionary appointment to teach English to children and youth in Bangkok, Thailand. The appointment would be for five months. I said I did not feel I could consider that long an assignment at this time.

Then they mentioned a similar mission for three months in Macau, China. I promised to examine the Concordia English Center Web site and pray about the Macau opportunity.

I really had to pray for guidance. Hazel said she did not feel she could go on such a mission so, if I went, I would have to go alone. I had to decide if I was ready to leave my wife of fifty-eight years for three months and invest thousands of dollars from our savings account to teach English and Bible studies on the other side of the world.

May 14, 2004: Today I logged on to the LCMS Web page and got a more detailed description of the missionary opportunity in Macau. I was surprised to find that it focused in large measure on the Lutheran School for Deaf Children in Macau. Interesting! My field for fifty or more years has been in education of deaf children. Hazel and I actually visited the Lutheran school in Macau about 1980 when I was attending a professional meeting in Hong Kong. I had no idea that the school and the Concordia English Center in Macau were functioning near to each other.

This was a development I had not anticipated. I had to decide if it was a signal that the school for the deaf might be a better place for me to further the kingdom. Was this the route I should be following in view of my background, experience, and faith? I wrote to the people in Macau and awaited their reaction.

While waiting for a reply from Macau, I heard from another overseas source with which I had made contact through a mutual friend.

May 15, 2004: Today I received an e-mail from Roberta Hill, a member of a missionary team associated with Trans World Radio located in Bratislava, Slovakia. I am not sure I even know where Slovakia is!

Roberta says they are trying to start a new educational center, the Bratislava Educational Resource Center (BERC), for the English-speaking children of American missionaries in that city. Her e-mail asks, "Do you happen to have any experience in education?"

Lord, what does this mean? You know that I have spent the last forty years of my life working in a variety of educational programs.

I took this subject to prayer and mailed off my resume to Roberta. Could this be what I should be doing with my education and managerial skills? Would Hazel understand and encourage me or discourage me?

May 16, 2004: Hazel has again said she will not go on a foreign mission, but she will not object if I feel called to go. Guide me, Lord, as to which direction I should follow to serve You and Your kingdom. I pray for the power of Your Holy Spirit to guide me. Not my will but Yours be done.

It was not easy to explain to my wife that I wanted to leave her for three months. It sounds now much worse than it was. I was not "leaving her" in the generally understood sense of dissolving our marriage but responding to a call from my Lord and heavenly Father for a relatively short period to respond to His call to service in another country.

Hazel understood, though her concern for my health and safety over such a long period was paramount in her mind.

> May 17, 2004: Lord, I am facing a situation where I must explain to my wife my feelings of being called to undertake a mission to further Your kingdom. I can relax and do nothing but attend Bible classes, attend church services, and carry ministry here in New Hampshire, or I can reach out and respond to an opportunity where my special talents and experience may be just what is needed somewhere else in the world.

I faxed my resume to Macau and got an immediate response from Sharon Owens, the head of the English center there. She asked if I wanted to teach English to Chinese children and adults or teach in the school for the deaf. I responded, "English to adults."

The questions were still there. Did I need to go five to ten thousand miles away from my wife, family, and home at great personal financial expense at this time of my life? Was I building up a phony case for foreign travel and calling it a missionary call?

> May 25, 2004: Roberta has sent about three more e-mails from Bratislava with her business plan, minutes of recent parent meetings, and other documents on the demographics of the area. I have had trouble downloading her attachments. Lord, does this mean You are saying I should not consider this idea any further? I decided to ask her to cut and paste the documents on an e-mail message which she did.

It was a hard decision to make on these two very interesting and equally challenging missionary opportunities. I would have liked to accept both of them, but of course, that was not possible. I was very impressed with the research and planning that Roberta Hill had done in

Bratislava. With much prayer, and after discussion with Hazel, I finally made my decision.

> July 5, 2004: I have accepted the call to go to Slovakia! So here I am, Lord, preparing for a three-month overseas assignment to begin on August 25. I will fly to Vienna and then be driven to my apartment in Bratislava. I have my airline tickets. I'm going! Last week a friend at church quietly pressed a roll of ten $100 bills in my hand to help with my expenses on the upcoming mission. Thank you, Lord.

The decision seemed to be an ideal opportunity for me. I would be going to help an interested group of parent missionaries organize an English language educational program for their children in mid-Europe. We would have to use classrooms and teaching staff available in Bratislava, distance learning through the Internet, and home schooling by the parents. Many residents in Slovakia use German, and that matched my limited, but adequate, conversational skills in German.

If I could have chosen an assignment and a location I do not believe I could have done better than what the Lord had prepared for me. Bratislava is close to Vienna but much less expensive than Vienna. I could travel to Vienna by fast train or bus from Bratislava whenever desired.

I spent three months in Slovakia and found it very rewarding. The BERC program was off and running by September 15 and has survived and grown since then. The parents were delighted to have a good educational program in a Christ-centered environment and at a cost that was within their missionary budgets. God had truly opened the doors to this opportunity. I felt a little like St. Paul when he traveled to a new mission area.

> When I went to Troas to preach the good news about Christ, I found that the Lord had already prepared the way. (2 Corinthians 2:12)

When I left Bratislava to come home in mid-November, 2004, the BERC program was moving ahead as planned. I met many wonderful people at the Evangelical Church of the Augsburg Confession (Lutheran) where I attended every Sunday. I also joined a mid-week Bible study at the pastor's apartment, which was enriching.

Among my colleagues at TWR were two young women journalists, Mariellyn and Wallyce, who sort of adopted me as their substitute grand-father. We had apartments across the hall at the missionary residence house that we called Sonshine House. They watched over me much as Hazel would have had she been there, so in many respects their presence and daily concern relieved some of Hazel's lingering concerns for my health and well-being. I had no trouble thanking God that He had placed these fine young Christian women as my neighbors.

My good wife and two of our daughters, Carol and Joyce, flew to Vienna and spent ten days with me visiting Vienna, Budapest, and Bratislava. Hazel and the girls had a chance to meet my colleagues at BERC, including Wallyce and Mariellyn, visit the famous cities of Vienna, Budapest, and Bratislava, and of course enjoy the sights and the cuisine for which these cities are world famous.

I felt that this had been the right choice at this time in my life. The BERC educational program strengthened the missionary programs in that area, and that confirmed for me that this was indeed what God wanted me to do in 2004.

In 2005, I responded to the earlier invitation from the Concordia English Center, a mission of the Lutheran Church-Missouri Synod, to go to Macau, China, for seven weeks to teach English as a Second Language to Chinese adults. Once again, I went off alone into unknown territory while my good wife kept the home fires burning in Keene, New Hampshire. I tutored Chinese businessmen and women in English. Most of these students came from the enormous gambling industry in Macau, sometimes called the Las Vegas of the East.

Most of my time, however, was directed to teaching English Bible study at no charge to small groups of college students, businessmen and women, retired engineers, secretaries, waitresses, and housewives. Our Bibles were in both English and Chinese. Students were grouped according to their proficiency in English, so when the students were just beginners, I had an interpreter to help.

By first building a friendly relationship with the group by sharing information about family, jobs, sports, and recreational preferences, I found it possible to introduce the gospel of Jesus Christ in a natural and non-threatening way. I felt especially blessed to have this opportunity at age eighty to reach out to those who had not heard of the God of Abraham, Isaac, and Jacob and the only Son he sent to redeem us 2,000 years ago.

Back in New Hampshire, I have been involved in a week-long Joni and Friends Family Retreat for families with disabled members. I meet regularly for Bible study and prayer with groups of inmates at a local prison and have found that My Problem Cards have been well received by men facing long periods away from their families and friends. I have organized and taught Sunday School classes for developmentally delayed men and women in New Hampshire and in Florida where we spend the winters. God has indeed blessed me with many opportunities to further His kingdom and the personal resources of health and motivation to accept His offer to serve.

Chapter 15 ✌

Epilogue: Reflections

Then I heard the voice of the Lord saying, "Whom shall I send? And who will go for us?" And I said, "Here am I. Send me!" (Isaiah 6:8)

On November 30, 1946, Hazel and I were married at the First Methodist Church in Schenectady, New York. We spent several of our honeymoon days in Colonial Williamsburg, Virginia, at the Williamsburg Lodge where we were able to get a room we could afford on my salary of forty-two dollars a week as a junior electrical engineer with the Western Electric Company.

We returned to Williamsburg in November 2006 to celebrate our sixtieth wedding anniversary and Thanksgiving Day with our family members. Our three daughters attended this wonderful celebration with members of their families:

- Carol Fellendorf Barbierri and Richard Barbierri, D.D.S.
  - Cara Barbierri, Ph.D.
  - Cody Barbierri
- Linda Fellendorf Mousavi and Hossein Mousavi
  - Ramin Mousavi and Aimee Armour Mousavi
  - Kamran Mousavi and Beth Krandel Mousavi

- Brandon George Mousavi, great grandson, DOB 1/19/2007
- Joyce Fellendorf Jackson and J. Craig Jackson, M.D.
  - Collin Jackson
  - Ashley Jackson

Carol is the founder, and now executive director, of Arlington Area Child Care, Inc (Happy Days Play School) in Arlington, Vermont. Linda, who lives in Mesa, Arizona, is a caregiver in group homes for persons with various disabilities. Joyce is president and CEO of Northwest Kidney Centers (NKC) based in Seattle, Washington, the first out-patient kidney dialysis program in the world. NKC is a model for saving and sustaining the lives of people with chronic kidney disease.

We showed the family 8mm silent movies taken on our wedding day and then movies of the first steps taken by each daughter. Other film selections included family holiday gatherings with relatives and friends, most of whom have long since moved on to their heavenly home. We enjoyed the fellowship, as it provided an opportunity to reflect on the blessings God had showered on our family over the years. Grandson Ramin made a video with his new Canon camcorder, a recent gift from family members in anticipation of the arrival of Brandon George Mousavi, our first great-grandchild.

My Problems, God's Solutions mentions just a few of the many experiences we have had in the last fifty years of our marriage. We have literally hundreds of these cards describing our journey of faith in a loving God who has guided us and enabled us to handle issues that at times seemed insurmountable. We hope and pray that others will be as blessed as our family has been over the years knowing that a living and loving God will provide answers to every problem in His own time and in His own way.

I need to mention one caution to the reader who has persevered to this point in my book. There are some problems and solutions that may best be forgotten. So while recording problems at the time may be fruitful in getting solutions and is still highly recommended, there are some cards that you may want to destroy rather than save. "Forgive and forget" at times may be better than remembering a problem and the personal circumstances associated with it. Our Lord Jesus demonstrated this many times in scripture and we could not do better than to follow His example.

Long ago I heard a story which illustrates my point. A young migrant worker reported to her priest that she had met Jesus in the field where she was picking tomatoes and spoken to him. The priest passed it off as a dream at first, but each week the girl came back with the same report. Finally, he said to the girl, "The next time you speak with Jesus, ask him to tell you what sins I confessed to him that morning. If he can tell you what I said in my private prayer of confession, I will believe that you have really seen him."

A week later the girl showed up again at church. The priest asked, "Well, did you see Jesus again and ask him the question I suggested?" The girl responded, 'Yes, I did as you told me, father. I asked him what sins you had confessed that morning and he said, 'I forgot'."

I would like to acknowledge my gratitude to George Dillaway, Project Manager at WinePress Publishing, Enumclaw, Washington, and his capable staff for their cooperation in preparing this book. In addition, I want to express gratitude to my friend, Bettie L. Donley, former publication director at the Alexander Graham Bell Association for the Deaf, for her encouragement and editorial support services in preparing the manuscript for publication.

Last but by no means least, I want to express my love and gratitude to my beloved Hazel, who has survived sixty years as my wife and shared in the planning and the carrying out of all of the missions to which the Lord has called me.

Printed in the United States
79161LV00003B/281